Confessions Of A Real 'CB' Nut

by
Bob Holt

Writers Club Press
San Jose · New York · Lincoln · Shanghai

Published by Writers Club Press, an imprint of iUniverse.com, Inc.

For information address:
iUniverse.com, Inc.
620 North 48th Street
Suite 201
Lincoln, NE 68504-3467
www.iUniverse.com

URL: http://www.writersclub.com

DEDICATION

To:

Crackerjack, Nighthawk, MONKEYWRENCH, Pipeman, STOREMAN and Insurance Man

Without you, the "CB" experiences shared in this book would not have taken place and I would not have had the opportunity to have enjoyed your friendship. Gentlemen; "Good Buddies," thank you for the special memories.

73'S

Country Cousin

"HOOK, LINE, AND SINKER:

When did I really get hooked? Let's see, it was in late November of 1974. Until then I'd never heard of Citizen's Band Radio. My life was pretty normal. Del and I had been married twelve years, no children. According to Del, I'm child enough for anyone. I've been with the same company for twelve years traveling northeastern North Carolina for a food service equipment company. Del's a beautician, operating a one stall shop beside the house.

We'd met by chance back in 1961 when she stepped off a bus across the highway from where I was working. I was really sitting in front of the Houston's ESSO waiting for someone to drive up wanting gas. Remember those days when someone pumped it for you? When she stepped off, I almost fell out of the chair. God, she was beautiful. Dressed in heels, her white polka-dot dress just set off her gorgeous black hair. She walked into the café beside the bus station. It won't really a bus station, Simmon's was sorta like a mini strip mall with a fish market, a convenience mart that served as a bus station too, a tire recapping center and café. Bryan and Kathleen Simmons had operated the complex for years. Really more Kathleen than Bryan. He had an absolute affinity for booze. Spent a lot of his time enjoying just that. He'd get on a binge that would last for weeks at the time. I remember one night being awakened by loud knocking at the back door. It was just after 2 AM. Who in the world could it be at this hour? There stood Kenneth Smith. Actually he was swaying back and forth more than standing. We'd been class mates through high school.

"Bobby, we need a tractor."

"For what?"

He smelled just like "the day after".

"We're in the ditch over by the grave yard."

I walked with him down through the field beside the house and came out on the dirt road. Just like he said, they were in the ditch. I walked up to the car and opened the door. Yep, smelled just like Kenneth. Bryan and another guy were all crumpled up in the back seat and there was something that might have passed for a woman, only on a moonless night when you were blindfolded, slumped down in the front. Having told Kenneth I'd be back shortly, I walked back to the house and started back to bed. Momma had said many, many times that there won't nothing good that happened after midnight. She certainly was right this time.

"Honey, what was that all about?"

"Some damn drunk said he'd gone off the road into the ditch."

"What did you do?"

"I went with him to see. He was right."

"What are you going to do?"

"Go back to bed. Not my problem. They didn't ask me to help em get drunk. "

I never heard anything else out of the them. The car was gone the next morning.

Why Kathleen put up with him was a mystery. My brother, Ronnie, next to me married their daughter a couple of years after Del and I and he fitted right in with the drinking. He'd had a pretty rough childhood suffering from what was termed a "Blue Baby". Having several holes in his heart made if impossible for him to fully develop. Didn't slow him down none when it came to smoking and drinking. We'd steal a pack of Momma's cigarettes, Pall Malls, those long ones without filters, real cigarettes, and go into the woods behind the house. We'd fire up as many as we could hold between our fingers, at least six at the time. We'd get sick as dogs sometimes. That happened mostly when we were desperate and rolled our own. We'd use the left overs in the pack house in the winter and spring, and the good stuff when it was there. Taking a golden leaf that was "in order", meaning just moist enough to be handled, and rolling it like a cigar was by far the best substitute, excuse me, that won't a substitute, that was the real stuff. Rabbit tobacco was the last choice. Smoking or chewing it would knock your socks off. Especially if you swallowed some of the juice. We tried corn shucks, but couldn't keep the flames down. Taking a big puff on one of those baby's would get the hairs on your tonsils burned off. I guess it was like Dave Gardner said on one of his records. We'd smoke chains if we could light them. Bless your heart, there's another testimony. After we were "full growed", Momma would tell us she'd think the tall shrubbery out by the highway was on fire before she realized we were out there waiting for the school bus. We thought we'd hidden those columns of smoke better than that. My tree house in the huge oak tree by the corn crib and stables was my favorite place to smoke in the summer. I could have had fifty going at one time and the smoke would have disappeared into the canopy. That same oak tree took Del and my full attention each year at Thanksgiving just to rake leaves. Forth of July was freezing corn, on and off the cob, but this was different. Rake, rake, rake and burn, burn, burn, all day long with nothing to show that night but tired muscles and lots of blisters. At least with the corn, there was the joy of eating the fruits of our labor.

If we could find their booze, we'd get into that too. If we couldn't find theirs, with hollowed out reeds in hand, we'd head for closest liquor still we knew about at the time. There were times when we would wait for hours before the opportunity to drink out of the mash barrels would come. If the bootlegger's were using horse manure to speed up the fermentation process, we'd find another one. Junior Had more guts than us. He'd swipe a whole gallon jar of the finished product. Now folks, we could get drunk for a month on a gallon of white lightening. We'd spend hours out in the woods sipping on something and talking about girls mostly and what we thought we knew about them. Sally Jo, the gal with the big knockers was the topic of discussion often. Lynn knew somebody she'd showed them to. We were all sure we wanted to be next. The older boys would be there sometimes, especially if we had the good stuff and they'd tell us sex stories that was hard to imagine, but we sure tried. I got into Branch Miller's white lightening one time and it sure lit up my life. Junior, Lynn and me we going go the mill swimming and took the short cut around the barn to the dirt road. Branch lived in Mr. Jamie's Southerland's tenant house just across the road. He was sitting on the edge of the porch drinking something. We walked over and he offered us a sip. It looked like grape wine. I turned the gallon jar up and took a great big swig. When that stuff hit the bottom, my breath and voice were gone. Branch almost rolled off the porch.

"Good stuff ain't it."

Finally I could talk.

"What in the hell is in that."

That warm feeling set in almost immediately. It tasted like cherries and was real sweet. Once the fire was out, it tasted good. Branch had taken a gallon of the good stuff, (I was always told that if you took a jar of it and moved it around some. The good stuff would have little beads dancing on the surface.) and poured a jar of pitted cherries in it. after sitting for a couple of weeks, he strained it. the cherries would no longer be red, all that coloring would be in the booze along with the cherry taste. If you really wanted to put somebody's lights out, give them the cherries. I've heard stories of those things ending up in a salad that was served at the "Dinner on the Grounds after Church" get together. Those little old "holier than thou ladies" would get snockered and never would know what hit them.

One time Momma and Daddy were gone to Kinston and we found a pint of Kentucky Gentleman. Being great western fans, we sat up a bar in the kitchen. I'd pour Ronnie a big one pretended to do the same for me. He drank the whole pint and friends, what followed, won't pretty. First he got wilder than hell, then he got sick, God he got sick, throwing up on everything. The kitchen, living room, bathroom, everything. Finally he passed out. I knew if they got home before I cleaned up the mess, my ass was grass and the mowing machine won't far behind. I could hear that big wheel Yazoo warming up. After the mess was up, I tried to pour hot coffee in him. Then I drug him into the bathroom, filled up the tub with cold water and dumped him in. Little by little, he came around. I'd never pull that crap again. It won't worth it. Oh, he'd had his moments like the time he threw the butcher knife through the screen door because I wouldn't let him in. Luckily it stuck right in the crack of my "come together" missing the meat and jewels completely. Then there was the time he shot me with the air rifle, OK, we were having a war and he won.

Cause I was the biggest, I got blasted for everything. Nah, ain't no way I could have done all those things. Won't enough time in the day.

When Ronnie was eighteen, the doctors said open heart surgery was his only hope. The operation procedure was still in its infancy and the chances of survival were no better than 50%. He won't real thrilled about that. In fact, he just plain disappeared the day before he was scheduled to check in at Chapel Hill. I knew where he was but couldn't get the crowd at Benny's pool hall to understand the gravity of the situation. The sheriff's department did though. I found out later that he was hiding behind a couch when I walked in trying to find him. I always figured the reason they wouldn't help was because of all those times I'd played pool with Benny or his father, Sam. Sam spoke with a lisp and we all called him, Sham. I couldn't play worth a damn, you better not put any money on the table with either of my brothers, they'd clean you out, but I sure could fram the hell outta the balls and holler "Luck". They'd get madder than hell cause I'd win.

After the operation, he wasn't allowed to move, turn over or get up for months. Now you're up the day after. It was a big success and he entered a two year business college that fall. He took one of those early retirement packages from IBM several years ago and is studying to be a minister now. I guess with all that experience behind him, he should make a good one.

My younger brother, THE MISTAKE! Oh yes he was. Back in 1947, Momma and Daddy made their final trip back to the Big Apple to reminisce about days gone by. They'd gone there in 1937 and Daddy operated a filling station. He loved telling the stories about the gangsters and how they'd pull up to the pumps, get out and walk around while he filled the big touring car's tank with gas, checked the oil and cleaned the windshield. You never tried any small talk, just get the job done, collect the money and they'd be on their way.

They came back home when my sister was born in 1939, returned, staying til April of 1941 when my grandmother died. They decided to stay at the old home place since I was due to arrive in June.

During the trip something musta gone bad wrong because few months later, Momma began to swell. How's that little ditty go? Three months later, all was well, six months later, she began to swell, nine months later, out he came, Larry Maxwell Holt doing his thing. Yeah, yeah, I know, that's just a little different from the way I remember it too.

Some mistake, he has his Ph.D. and is a professor at Rollins College in Rockledge, Florida teaching something about "Applied Computer Technology" or something like that. Doc. ain't doing bad, forth or fifth marriage, who knows anymore. This last one was through the miracle of advertisement. They met through an ad he placed in the local paper and Amber set his fields on fire. When we were down to watch him receive his doctorate, she told us that after two weeks of waiting, she took him down in the bathroom and showed him the joys of life. She shared that with everyone that was present at the party the night before commencement. I think she'd been in the jar of "good stuff", no, it didn't have any cherries, just lots of beads, Mr. Luther had sent down. Larry just walks around with a big smile now. A lot of water has

6

gone under his bridge, like the time he trashed his 57 Chevy at Maxwell's Mill. He'd been on a hot date with his childhood sweetheart, Annette, and was running late. Momma always told us what time to be home, usually 10:30 on week nights and midnight on weekends. He'd topped the hill and started down the other side, lost control and rolled it several times. Luckily he had nothing but scratches and bruises. Looked a whole lot worse than he was. Being covered with blood makes you look that way. He walked the last ½ mile home and woke Daddy up standing at his bedside and turning the light on. Scared hell outta Daddy. Took a minute or two to figure out who he was. More about him later.

Where am I? Oh, back to our meeting. I hollered telling Houston I'd be back and walked across the highway, Del, it's Ruby Adele but she didn't like Ruby or the way us southerner's said Adele. It would come out sounded like Aaaaaaadele instead of Ah'del, so she chopped it down to Del. Won't a whole lot you could do to screw that up. Like me and Bobby, there would always be those that would insist on calling her, Aaaaaaaadele, was sitting at the first table just inside the door. I walked pass and took the closest table with a good view. Connie walked over and took my order; burger, fries and Pepsi. Just as I was beginning to enjoy the view, in walked Mac Batchelor and set down with her. That bastard, who the hell did he think he was? That's my woman. Or least she was going to be. Just as Connie brought my order, they got up a left. I ain't sure if I finished or even started on my food. I spent the balance of the day trying to figure out were I'd seen her.

"Damn! That's where."

I set up in the bed. It was just after 3 AM.

"She's Mac's sister!"

Mac had shown a bunch of us guys her picture several months back telling us what a good looking sister he had. He was sure right about that. She was sitting on the edge of a bed, black dress, heels, couple strings of pearls with her hair pulled up on top of her head in a twist, ruby red lips, God!

Next day I called Carol Jean Marady and asked if she knew Mac's sister. Yes, she'd graduated with her in 1958.

"Take me to meet her."

"OK, we'll do it Friday night."

God, it was Wednesday, why couldn't we go now? I'd have to wait. She had other plans.

After what seemed like several months, Friday evening finally arrived. I pulled up along side Carol Jean at Rhodes' Grill in Beulaville. She motioned for me to come ride with her. She'd called Del and asked if she would like to join us for burgers. She was sitting on the front porch when we arrived. The light blue dress was perfect for her beautiful black hair and those ruby red lips………. Yeah, yeah, give me a minute. I knew right then this was the woman I wanted to marry. OK, it might have been "heat" cause I sure was hot. Those primordial fires were raging inside. Whatever it was, I wanted her. As they say, "the rest is history."

We moved back to the country the third year we were married. Our social life up to this point consisted of going Church on Sunday, I was teaching the Adult class at Sunday School, visiting Bo and L.C. Southerland, he was superintendent of our Sunday School and Bo was the piano player, our closest friends to play cards, watch TV and once in a while go out to eat. In the earlier years, we'd get together with Johnny Bill Jenkins and Barbara along with Roger and Eleanor Harper often continuing a friendship started when we moved to Pink Hill. I'd known Roger, "Chipmonk", for years. His 54 ford, the "Blue Goose" created memories that will stay with me forever. This ain't the place to talk about some of them. He'd come by the house several nights a week and we'd go to the Hillview Café in Pink Hill. That was the gathering place for teenagers. If you had a hot date, pulling around the side in the dark, we called that; "Rabbit Hill"., was the place to be. Otherwise J. W. Grady or one of the other car hops would take care of your order.

"Give me a Hamburger; 25 cents, fries; ten cents, and pepsi (fountain drink); ten cents."

That's 45 cents, can you believe it? I know, that was back before time began in the fifties. In 1950, pepsi's were a nickel and candy bars, big ones, were too. When pepsi's went to six cents, we won't ever going to drink another one. History will tell you that didn't happen. J. W. would become a short order cook later. I guess that's when he starting mixing orders and instructions up. Later when he became an outside sales representative for Grady's and then Blizzard Building Supply, you knew when he said he'd drop by or the delivery truck would, neither would. "Tiny Town" was another hang out. Bob and Nellie Hughes ran a pretty tight ship offering a place to eat and dance to the music of the juke box in the back room. Car hops would take your order on the outside offering the opportunity to sit around the side and "neck". I spent lot of time playing duces wild or Dr. Pepper with Bob. Of course the back room was the big drawing card. There'd always be a few singles in there.

Roger joined the Air Force when he graduated from high school and trained as an aircraft mechanic. Spending most of his tour in the South Pacific in the 110 degree F. shade really did a number on his internal thermostat. That won't all it did either, but I won't speculate. He walked into a spinning prop on the tarmac one night that cut his nose off plus doing lots of other damage. The Plastic Surgeons put him back together and when he returned home, he looked no worse for the wear. He'd stand beside you in 80 degree F. temperatures shivering. A year back home took care of that and Eleanor did the rest. Pepsi's, cigarettes, Barbara and Kathy along with plenty of food lit up Johnny Bill's life. Eating was what we did best when we got together too. Eating too much was expected and we'd all be miserable trying to play cards afterwards. It was certainly a fun time though. Johnny Bill left this life much too early. Other than getting together with a small group from church to cook out, That was about it. We didn't really get to know our neighbors because of the type of work I do. I'd be out of town most of the week. Changes in my territory had just begun to allow me more nights at home.. Enough of that. Thirty three years old, a little over-weight, doing great, just got my first Thunderbird. All my marbles were in the same jar until…….

"Bobby, Bo's on the phone, wants us to go over and play cards."

"Okay, tell her we're on the way."

When we went in, Bo had the table set up for cards. L.C. had just taken a shower after coming in from the chicken houses. They have a poultry farm, raising hatching eggs under contract. Bo works at DuPont in Kinston. Anyway he was sitting in the kitchen listening to some kind of radio. I walked over and listened too. It sounded as if two or three guys were talking on the phone, except they were calling each other funny names. L.C. said they were using CB lingo and those funny names were handles. He told me the boys talking were over around Beulaville. Thats about fifteen miles away. They sounded just like they were in the room with us. L.C. said the radio was a new fad that was becoming real popular. He'd just gotten one about two weeks ago. It was a Royce 1-620 with a handheld microphone. We went outside and he tried to show me the CLR-2 antenna in the gum tree. I could see it's outline shining in the moonlight.

Back inside, he picked up the mike and broke in on the conversation. He called himself the "Crackerjack". He'd talked to these fellows before and knew some of them personally. I said hello to "Pipe Man", "Store Man", and "Cricket Man". That was about all I did say because I couldn't understand what they were talking about. They kept saying,

"Roger, 10-4, Roger 4, Negatory".

"Cricket Man" was telling "Crackerjack", he was blowing smoke, walking tall, wall to wall, 10-8, 10-10, all that sounded like Greek to me. "Pipe Man" kept calling "Store Man" a "Rachet Jaw" or something. They sounded as if they were having a ball. "Crackerjack" said good night to all and signed off saying something like…."KIR 1638, Crackerjack 10-7, 10-27 to 1-1. Night all. He'd sent for his license much earlier and already had them.

He told me about the radio in the pick-up and how he could talk back to home from five to ten miles away. He was planning to put one in the car too. He kept talking about needing new whips, coax, bumper mounts and springs. I didn't have the slightest idea what he was talking about. It all sounded good though.

Where do I get one, how much and who installs it? A mobile was less than a hundred dollars, antenna twenty dollars and we could install it ourselves. I bit….Hook, Line and Sinker!

Del finally got my attention saying something about it's past 1 AM, and time to go home. We usually left around eleven.

Needless to say, no visions of sugar plums dancing in my head that night. All I could see was radio, antenna, and me with mike in hand.

Stopping by Southeastern Radio the next day and looked at the CB's. I didn't try to buy one because Crackerjack's son-in-law, Max, knew someone there and could get them wholesale. That afternoon Max called and told me to come over, he had my radio. I flew over! Max showed me my brand new 1-600 Royce. She was a beauty. Three knobs, an on-off volume, squelch, and channel selector. We all three began the installation. Now, that was a job! Pulling the back-seat out, running the coax under the carpet, and where does the radio go? Ever own a Thunderbird? We mounted it just above the gas pedal under the dash. I couldn't see the channel selector because of the steering wheel but who cared? It was mounted. We hooked the hot wire to the fuse panel, only blew one fuse doing that. Now we were ready to try it out. Max and I started down the road leaving Crackerjack in his pickup at the egg house. She seemed to be doing fine.

"Crackerjack, how do you copy?"

"Chipmonk, you're five on the meter, sounds good."

We were three miles down the road and he was blowing us out of the car. We went to B. F. Grady School about five miles away.

"Crackerjack, how we doing?"

"Still sounds good, looks like we got it right. Come on back."
"10-4 Crackerjack, KIR 1638 unit three clear. 10-27 1-1."

Chipmonk told me about channel eleven being the call channel. Everybody listened to it for a call. Channel ten belonged to the truck drivers. They used it to tell each-other about the Smokeys (Highway Patrolmen).

That night after gulping dinner down, I went outside to see who was on the radio. Must have been about thirty degrees but who cared, people were talking on the radio. Wasn't hard to find Crackerjack. He was so close, he came in on all the channels. He was telling the guys about installing the rig on my car that afternoon and that I was probably listening in. They decided to call me "Traveling Man". I hollared

"Break."

Crackerjack came back.

"Go ahead Traveling Man. Give Pipe Man a Call."

"How bout it Pipe Man. Got a copy?"

"10-4 Traveling Man. You're 10-1, but I copy."

"Hey Traveling Man, stick that mike in your mouth and hollar in it."

"Okay Store Man, sound any better?"

"Roger, but you're still weak."

"Break Traveling Man, you copy Cricket Man?"

"10-4 Cricket Man."

"Traveling Man, you need a Power Mike on that mobile. Won't have to hollar then."

"10-4, what's that?"

"It's a souped up model, amplified to make you sound a whole lot louder. You'll be 10-8 then."

"10-4, preciate that, I'll get one tomorrow. Crackerjack, I'm freezing out here. 73's to all. Traveling Man 10-7."

Needless to say the next day I was looking for a power mike. None were to be found in Kinston so my search continued as soon as I arrived in Greenville. Asking for the nearest place to buy a power mike, I ended up at Pair Electronics.

"Yes sir, may I help you?"

 Stewart was trying to decide if he knew me.

"I'm looking for a power mike for my CB radio."

"All right sir. What kind do you want?"

"Kind, How many kinds are there?"

"There are hand helds, desk type, electronic switching, relay switching, noise canceling, all kinds."

"I just want one for the rig in my car."

Stewart brought out a Turner JM+2U. That was a sexy looking thing, but it didn't have a plug on the end of the cord.

"You have to wire it to fit the type of radio it's going on."

"Then I need a soldering iron."

"What kind?"

Here we go again.

"Stewart, just bring me what I need."

All right, I'll be back in a moment."

I should have walked out then and there. I didn't know what I was getting into.

"OK, here's all you need to wire it. You can use this Weller gun for lots of other jobs, a roll of solder, rosin type of course, a battery and the plug. What else can I do for you?"

"Putting it all together would help."

Stewart laughed.

"We don't do that. Let's see, one JM+2U; $65.00, one Weller gun, $17.95, one pound roll of solder; $4.00, one seven volt battery; $3.90, one four pin plug; $1.00. That's $95.52 including tax. Thank you sir. Have a good day."

"Breaker 1-1, KIR 1638 unit three calling base, Crackerjack you around?"

"Go ahead Traveling Man."

"Hey Crackerjack, got me a power mike today."

"10-4, got it on?"

"Negative, got to wire it."

"Know how?"

"Ain't got the slightest, but bought a soldering gun, solder, and plug. Wiring instruction's in the box with the mike."

"10-4, give me a hollar when you get it hooked up."

"Roger 4, KIR 1638, unit three clear."

"KIR 1638, base clear."

Have you ever tried to thread a needle with a rope? The end of the soldering gun looked like a light pole beside the pins on the plug. Every time I tried to solder one wire it stuck to at least two pins or another wire. I finally got it. Three hours later, one pound of solder, and half a roll of black tape. It took ten minutes to get the plug cover over all that tape. Now I was going to be 10-8. I ran to the car and plugged it in. You never heard such squealing in your entire life. It keyed by itself and sounded like it was going to blow up. Back to the bench. When all else fails, read the instructions. White wire on one, shield on two, black on three, red on four. That ain't the way the original one was wired. OK, I'll do it their way.

"Hey, this thing works!"

Whistle in it and she pegs the needle.

After supper, back to the car. Tonight they'll hear me.

"Break Pipe Man, how am I sounding tonight?"

"Traveling Man, you're 10-8, get that power mike?

"10-4, a JM+2U Turner, just got it wired."

"Sounds like you got a foot warmer."

"Store Man, what in the world is that?"

Laughing, "You tell him Cricket Man."

"Evening Traveling Man. Its a power booster. It boosts your signal way up. But! Its illegal."

"Cricket Man, you got one?"

"Not me! Pipe Man does."

"Hey, not me, that's against the law."

"Aw Pipe Man, show him how it works."

"OK Traveling Man, look at your meter. What am I putting on it?"

"Looks like about 2db."

"OK, how bout now?"

"Looks like six db's"

"Now."

"Wow, you're in the RED!!!!!"

"Laughing, Okay, that's how it works."

"Crackerjack, you got one of those things?"

"Negative Traveling Man, not yet."

"Pipe Man, where'd you get it?"

"Ordered it out of a catalog."

"10-4. Crackerjack, lets order us one."

"Okay, soon."

"73's everybody, it's getting cold out here."

Next day between Oak City and Ahoskie, I heard two eighteen wheelers rag-chewing about antennas. They were saying two antennas were always better than one. They didn't mention anything about how they had to be mounted, (If there were closer than 9 feet, they would tend to be directional. With the antenna's mounted on the rear. They tended to hear better straight out the front.) just that they were better and "Big Mamma's" were the best. Oh, to have just missed that conversation, but I would have heard it somewhere else. I, of course, stopped by Pair Electronics on my way home.

"Yes sir, may I help you?"

Stewart hadn't learned to run when he saw me coming in the door yet, but he would.

"Stewart, I need two Big Mamma's for my trunk."

He didn't have them and tried to sell me what I really needed.

"The Hustler HQ 27's or the Shakespeare 173's co-phased will work better."

No way, that's not what those truckers were talking about, and they oughta know. I'd learn to listen to Stewart one day, but not yet.

I stopped in Kinston at Southeastern. Joe Butts would also learn to run from me.

"May I help you sir?"

I'd been standing there an hour, busiest place I'd ever seen.

"Two Big Mamma's for trunk groove mounting please."

Now the way I said that, Joe didn't question it. Had he known what I was going to do with them, he would have tried to stop me.

"All right sir, what else?"

"An SWR meter."

Another hundred dollars gone. The beginning of many. When I got home, I was going to install these babies myself.

"Crackerjack, how do you get both ends of the coax into the radio?"

"Traveling man, what are you talking about?"

"I got these two "Big Mamma" antennas mounted on the trunk and got the 2 pieces of coax run to the radio. How do I plug them in?"

I had already mounted the antennas and run the two pieces of coax under the carpet. Never occurred to me that the two ends wouldn't fit into one receptacle. Crackerjack said I needed a "T" and thought he had one. I drove over to the egg room. We spent the rest of the afternoon hooking them up.

"What's wrong the standing wave? Won't come below a three to one."

We trimmed the whips, nothing, if anything, worse.

Bo threatened to throw L.C.'s supper out if he didn't come to the house. We gave it up for the day. Only been working on it for four hours. No talking that night. I couldn't hear anybody but Crackerjack.

Next day I stopped by Southeastern again. Joe said I should have explained how I was going to use the antennas. I didn't need that type, they should have been co-phased. What now, since I'd already messed these up? A co-phasing harness was the only answer. Co.-phased, where'd I heard that before? Maybe Stewart, at Pair's.

I came home early, went to Crackerjack's and helped him get up the rest of the eggs. Bo and Max were working 4 to 12. L.C.'s daughter, Sandi would be fixing supper and she'd wait until we were finished. We ended up with a handful of PL 259's, adapters, and barrel connectors on it, but it worked. Well, better anyway, SWR was down to 1.7 to 1. Sandi had been down twice checking on us. Don't know why, it was only 9PM. Lucky for me, it was Del's late night in the shop. She'd been too busy to miss me.

A few weeks later we heard that the big coax worked better than the small. L.C. wanted to mount two 102" stainless steel whips on the pickup. We decided to use the big coax for that. Back to the rope and needle. Working with RG 8 U in a mobile was something else. It won't fit in tight places and the ends drive you nuts trying to solder them, especially when the wind's blowing. We finally got them mounted, "T" connector, antenna matchers, RG 8 U big coax, and anything else that would help. It worked pretty good. Still won't right, SWR was too high. Nobody could tell us why. We just didn't ask the right people. By the way, "big & little coax performance don't even come into play under 50 feet. In VHF, UHF and beyond, it does.

By now, walking into the egg room was dangerous. You couldn't get into the door without tripping over CB junk or coax and the pile was growing.

Still sitting in the car each night was leading to a foregone conclusion. I had to have a base station. It was cold in that car and I just wasn't getting out far enough. Del told me I could get one for Christmas. Into the catalogs I went. Which catalogs? For CB gear?????? OK, OK, Sears, J. C. Penny, Montgomery Ward? They had everything else and they had terms. After what seemed like hours of searching, there she was, in an Alden catalog. A Cobra 139; AM, SSB, NB, ANL, Dynamike, Squelch, Delta Tune, RF Gain, Clarafier, everything! What more could a person want? I didn't know what half of those things were, but I knew I needed them. Just below it, a Super Scanner Antenna. Electronic switching beam with 8 db gain. Just what I needed. I ordered both that night. I didn't mention the five hundred bucks to Del. That might have ended my future in CB then and there.

Sure enough, two weeks later it came. The back order slip. It would be after Christmas before either would be shipped. I was destroyed. How could I ever wait that long?

Crackerjack, or was it Bo?, decided to move his base from the kitchen to the living room. He needed about fifty more feet of RG 8 U, notice how I'm using all these numbers now. I've got this thing figured out. Crackerjack decided to bury the coax from the base of the tree to the house. We also installed a lightening arrestor in it for protection. When the coax was all in place, he checked the SWR and it had changed. Now, picture this, we're sitting in the middle of Bo's living room floor, wrenches, cutters, soldering iron, solder, SWR bridge and radio. She oughta shot both of us. There we were, checking, trimming ¼ to ½ inch of coax, checking again, cutting again. You can't change the SWR that way!

"EVERYBODY WANTS TO TALK TO SOMEBODY"

What seems so surprising about CB was that all these people were talking to each other. They wouldn't dream of talking to each other on the street. In fact most would shun each other under different circumstances. On CB everybody's a good buddy.

Need help? Broken down? Need a little information? Just key the mike.

"Breaker 1-0, need a little help."

"Go ahead breaker, you've got Peter Gun"

"Preciate the come back Peter Gun. You got the Blue Bird."

"I'm 10-7 on 1-7 about four miles south of Little Washington. Need some go juice. 10-4?"

"10-4 Blue Bird, just passed you northbound. You on the blue four wheeler south of the bear den?"

"10-4, that's me."

"10-4, stand by."

"Peter gun, if you can't help, I'll give him a hand."

"No problem, preciate it though. Be right back Blue Bird."

About fifteen minutes passes.

"Hey Blue Bird, Peter Gun headed your way. Had a little problem finding a can."

"10-4 Peter Gun, preciate it."

"Looks like you got plenty of help Blue Bird."

"10-4, they came from everywhere."

Three four wheelers, and one eighteen wheeler all wanting to help. Peter Gun spent thirty minutes just to help someone he'd never seen and probably never would again. That's CB'ers for you. Blue Bird might have been there hours if it hadn't been for the "Charlie Brown." For years since WW2 we've been building a wall around ourselves. Between TV and being too busy to be bothered, we've let ourselves get out of touch with each other. Remember when Mom and Dad put everybody in the car for a weekend or week at Grandma's or Aunt Lizzie's? Not any more, too busy. We used to have tobacco tyings or corn huskings, anything to get together with the neighbors to visit or help each other. Not anymore. Too many things to do just to keep our own heads above the water. Now both have to work, put the kids in pre-school, kindergarten or whatever, rush to work, rush home, mow the grass or the neighbors will talk. She's fixing supper, or was she too busy tonight, Kentucky Fried again. She had to wash and dry the clothes, or you'd be raising hell in the morning. Let's see now, take a shower, one small drink (in a sixteen oz. Glass) of whatever cranked or uncranked you, favorite chair, paper….

"Honey, turn to channel seven, I wanta watch the ball game."

Nine out of ten times, "lights out". "Where the hell did the evening go?" Too tired to do anything. Visiting? Absolutely not, they wanta see us let'em come over here.

As I said before, neighbors? I didn't know them. We didn't have anything in common. They farmed, worked at the local stores or factories. I sold commercial kitchen equipment. My day didn't begin until I was fifty miles from home. Three nights a week in a motel, I didn't want to go anywhere on the weekend. Del just got used to it.

Now I was beginning to meet and renew acquaintances with the neighbors. People I hadn't spoken to in fifteen years suddenly reappeared. Sure seemed good just to say hello again. Then there are those I never would have had the pleasure or opportunity of knowing. That made all of the " Flying Green Stamps" worthwhile. Monkey Wrench, Grandma, Green Six, Blue Dragon, Night Hawk, Speed Queen, Pipe Man, Store Man, of course Crackerjack, Little Bo Peep, Miss Kitty and Chipmonk. There are so many, they and their XYL's (wives) have given us many many hours of pleasure that never would have been otherwise.

The trips we took were a lot more enjoyable. Running with the pack, front door, back door or in the rocking chair. Time just disappeared. Fourteen hour trips to Nashville, Tennessee just floated by. Of course trying to keep the back door closed through the mountains was something else. Those eighteen wheelers knew every nook and cranny. They'd take those hair-pin curves at brake neck speed. Thats certainly how it looked to this "Flat Lander" I'd have to pass the microphone to Crackerjack riding shotgun. There was no way to drive and talk at the same time.

"Got a tight one up ahead Country Cousin, hold on." (Oh yes, by this time, the handle Country Cousin was born. I liked it much better than Traveling Man) Hold on I did, scared to death. That rascal up ahead was hauling forty thousand pounds, having a ball and I couldn't keep up. If you've never crossed the Great Smokey Mountains on US 40 at three in the morning bringing up the back door for three eighteen wheelers, you haven't lived.

"What's wrong Country Cousin, can't see your headlights no more. 10-4?" Eighty miles an hour and I couldn't keep up. The concrete divider looked as if it would come into the car with me any second. The massive stone face of the mountain daring me to get any closer.

"Crackerjack, tell that damn idiot we'll catch him on the next hill!!!"

If Del and Bo had been awake, the blood chilling screams would be heard throughout western Carolina and eastern Tennessee.

Sometimes the drivers would stop at the rest areas and we'd get a chance to "eyeball" them. Never met one we didn't like as much in person as on the radio. The eighteen wheelers were the greatest bunch of guys in the world. They'd do anything for you and save your cottonpicking neck if you'd let them. Think about that next time you're so close on the back door it looks as if you're trying to come in. Ever see that bumper sticker, " If you can't see my mirrors, I can't see you". Sure they sound ill sometimes. How would you sound if everytime you tried to use the phone for that important business call the operator kept coming into the conversation trying to patch other calls through. Hey, that's right, when they're out there, they're working. Most of us AIN'T. I know, you bought yours just like they did and you'll use any damn channel you please. Sure you will, but there are thirty eight other ones excluding channel 9. Wonder what's happening on them. Might be missing something. 10-4?

CB has done much more for the eighteen wheelers than just letting them know where that smokey bear with the picture taker is. It has let the public know what a great bunch of guys there are in those monsters we keep getting in the way of on the super slab.

"Good Buddy, bring yourself on, the front door's open."

Remember the last time you were behind one in a rainstorm? Couldn't see a damn thing, no way to get around him, had to though. Forty five crystallized miles per hour. Never will make that appointment like this.

"Hold on Good Buddy, front door's closed."

If he hadn't stopped you, you might have been looking at that "Big Base Station in the sky."

"OK, bring yourself on, she's open now."

What have we done for them? Wrapped the channel up for them of course. Approaching a town? Might as well cut the damn thing off. No way to talk over those base stations. Besides there are too many important things going on for the eighteen wheelers to use it anyway. We gotta know what "Sweet Thing" had for supper last night or be sure what time the party starts tonight. Can't move to another channel, somebody might call if they can get in between the "fastest keys in the world." Besides , ain't nobody going to walk on them anyway. A full gallon, beams, and a nonstop motor mouth.

Forget about them moving for us, OH! You didn't know that. 10-4, they moved from channel ten to nineteen a few years ago. That was to clear channel nine for us. I know I'm bellyaching about just a few operators. If all forty million operators didn't care, there'd be no CB.

"Breaker 1-9."

It was about 3 AM. The channel was dead. I was up looking for the "skip" to start. You could hear it begin on nineteen.

"Go ahead breaker, Country Cousin back."

"10-4 Country Cousin, you got the Barrel Bender. I'm about three miles east of Albertson on the triple ones. Three mules in the middle of the highway just standing there and the fog's beginning to roll in. Somebody gonna get killed. 10-4?"

"10-4 Barrel Bender. Stand by.

"The Sheriff's department monitored nine on a set the Duplin County CB Club gave them.

"Break Nine for the Sheriff's Department. KJR 4734, anybody copy?"

"You've got the Sheriff's Department, go ahead."

"10-4, I have an eighteen wheeler about three miles east of Albertson just before you get to B. F. Grady School. Say's there are three mules on the highway. Can you move them?"

"Stand by. OK, we've got a car headed that way."

"10-4, thanks. Breaker 1-9, Barrel Bender, County Mountys coming your way."

"10-4, OH HELL!!!!!! Look out!!! Cousin, we need a "Meat Wagon, semi just got two of them, jack-knifed!!!""

"Breaker nine for the Sheriff's Department. 10-33."

"Go ahead"

"Need an ambulance, eighteen wheeler just got two of the mules and bought the ditch."

Two or three minutes pass.

"The ambulance will ETA in about ten minutes. Our car should arrive any minute."

"10-4 , thank you sir. KJR 4734 clear."

"Break Barrel Bender, the meat wagon will ETA ten minutes. 10-4?"

"10-4 Cousin, buddy's checking on the driver now, preciate it."

The driver was hurt pretty bad. CB might have saved his life. I waited until the ambulance arrived before signing off. I heard on the news the next day that the driver was all right. Another feather in Mr. Eighteen Wheeler's and CB's hat.

"THE CART BEFORE THE HORSE"

I was copying the mail one day and ran across two guys talking about a fellow near Mount Olive called the "Bear Hunter" that had a "Box" for sale. Sounded just like what I needed. A hundred watts for a hundred dollars.

"Breaker 1-1 Crackerjack, you around?"

"10-4 Traveling Man, go ahead."

"10-27 - 5"

"Whatcha doing this afternoon?"

"Nothing, whatcha need?"

"Lets take a little trip. Tell you about it when I get to your 20. 10-4?"

"Roger Traveling Man, see you shortly. KIR 1638 Base clear."

"Unit three clear" My license still hadn't arrived, Base station either.

On the way to Beautancus I told Crackerjack what I'd heard and about how to get to Bear Hunter's twenty. When we got there he wasn't home. We rode around for a while chewing the rag with the Farmall Man near Faison. Later when we got back to Bear Hunter's he showed us the "box". She was a beauty, a Varmit 150. Three big knob's on the front of a big blue box. He said it worked fine, he just didn't need it. Say goodbye to five $20.00 bills.

Crackerjack laughed.

"You've got the cart before the horse."

He didn't know what I was thinking. Sure, my base station hadn't arrived. I dropped him off and rushed back home. After pulling the car as close to the back door as possible, I pulled a drop cord out to the car. You know, I forgot to ask Bear Hunter how to make this thing work. It looked simple enough, two connectors on the back, one marked "Ant." The other marked "radio". I plugged her in, hit the switch, nobody told me that thing had a fan! A few minutes later, after I calmed down, I turned to channel 23 and keyed the mike. The little red light came on. I started turning the knobs. It would get bright then dim, finally it was glowing cherry red. Must be ready.

"Breaker 1-1, anybody got a copy on the Traveling Man, downtown Albertson?"

"Roger Traveling Man, you got the Pole Cat in Wallace Town."

"Hey Pole Cat, I just got a new rig. How's it sound?"

"Cotton Picker, you're blowing smoke in downtown Wallace!"

"Whatcha running Traveling Man?"

"A Royce 1-600, power mike and two big mamma's on the trunk."

"Traveling Man, what did you say your twenty was?"

"Downtown Albertson at the home 20, on the mobile."

"Good buddy, you're running something besides a power mike on that mobile, you're putting 10 pounds on my meter."

Now you gotta understand I'm talking at least twenty five miles and I hadn't been able to get outta my underwear up to now.

"Polecat, I've got a little bit of help, what you running?"

"A Super Lynx, D-104 and Super Mag up ;about sixty feet."

"Breaker, Breaker, Breaker!!"

"Go A……Hea…….D, Breaker."

"Hey Traveling Man, don't you listen to that Polecat, he's got at least one thousand watts on that D-104."

"Cotton Pickin Blue Jay, you know I ain't got no such mess as that. (laughing)"

"You're tearing the needle outta my mess right now Polecat. Me sittin over here with my little Midland and you trying to blow it up."

They're both putting over ten pounds on me and I'm on the mobile.

"Hey Traveling Man, you're sounding good to be on a mobile. Whatcha got kicking it?"

"Varmit 150"

"That thing's for a base. You said you were on a mobile, 10-4?"

"Got a drop cord running to it Blue Jay."

"10-4, that's one way of doing it. It'll take a pretty long cord to use it though. Hi, Hi."

"See you fellers later, XYL calling, Blue Jay clear."

"OK Blue Jay, 73's, you too Pole Cat, I gotta go too. Traveling Man 10-7 the to house."

That night the guys said the rig sounded "10-8". It was really getting out. I made it to Jacksonville, Warsaw, Goldsboro, Pikeville and Snow Hill. I was really 10-8 for the first time.

This one guy kept hearing "breakers" I couldn't hear. In fact even after I got my new base and antenna he still had better ears than me. His setup was nice. A Lynx 23, D-104 with a little something extra. The little green box with a pre-amp gave him the "Big Ears". His antenna was only thirty or maybe forty feet up. Along with his location and pre-amp, his ears were something special. Goshean man kept saying, "Go ahead Break" when the rest of us could hear nothing. Even Gosheaneer living within eyeball distance couldn't pull out half what Frank was hearing.

Crackerjack was hearing lots of things I couldn't until I put my Super Scanner up. The mobile had good ears but nothing like a base station. I still had no concept about how radio waves worked.

Anytime a new station broke in, everybody tried to make the trip. If one of the fellows couldn't hear or be heard you can imagine the ribbing he took. "Alligator Station", all mouth and no ears.

When are you gonna get rid of that walki-talki and get something that'll talk. They could rip you apart.

"BASE STATION FINALLY"

My Cobra finally arrived the third week in January. Of course the antenna didn't. I picked up a cheap Ground Plane from Southeastern and mounted it on three 10 foot sections of TV mast. Anything to get on the air with the base.

A year before I had built an addition on the back of our "Double Wide". It measured 12' x 20' including the hall and utility room. The hall was on the same floor level with the "Double Wide and the rest of the addition was two steps down on ground level. I had built a little "Wet Bar" in the corner, sink and all. (The addition was originally designed to be a new kitchen. Before it was completed we had decided to build a much larger addition to include a Master Suite, Kitchen, Den and Bath and one half. It would have 1650 additional square feet.) The Cobra sat on the counter with the Varmit in the cabinet under it. Sure seemed good to be in the house plus Del could now hear all of the wonderful world of CB. We even gave her a handle. Crackerjack said it should be "Lady" since I called her that about half the time. She'd come down and listen but talk, NO WAY!!!! We'd try to get her into a QSO with Little Bo Peep or Pipe Lady, but all we'd get out of her was hello, yes, bye. Give her a telephone, that's different, she'd talk your ears off. Once in a while when we had friends over, we'd take the Turner +3 and sit it in the middle of the group on the floor. That way everybody could key it with their toe. We'd get her to talk that way.

I can't complain though, she certainly has tolerated a lot since I started CB'ing. She told a lot of folks we'd been married twelve years and it was the first time she knew I could talk. I had always said we could be happy together without running our mouths all the time. I didn't want to listen to all the Beauty Shop gossip anyway.

Besides, the CB was important. Look at all the technical aspects involved. Contribution to the destruction of the King's English was the most noticeable. One thing for sure, just listen to someone talking and right off you could tell how long they'd been on CB. The public schools spent twelve years trying to teach me how to talk and CB got rid of all that I learned to two weeks. If you wanted to talk, you did it "Their Way". How many Smokey reports could you get saying,

"Breaker Channel Nineteen. This is KJR 4734. I'm traveling South on Highway Eleven toward Kinston. I would appreciate any information concerning locations of Highway Patrolmen in the area."

Ain't nobody gonna answer someone talking like that. Probably the "Friendly Candy Company" anyway.

"Breaker 1-9 fer a eighteen wheeler north bound on 1-1. How's it look over your shoulder back toward K-town?"

"She's clean and green, ain't seen nothin, put the hammer down good buddy."

"Preciate that info good buddy. She be clean back to the Green City."

"10-4 Traveling Man, the Beaver Eater gonna be doing it this'a way."

See what I mean, isn't that much better. 10-40-Roger-4 Good Buddy. Thats a BIG 10-4!

Lets see, I got off track here somewhere, Oh, base station in the house. That's what we were talking about. Thing's really began to change with the rig in the house. Even with the cheap ground plane, getting out was much easier. All those hard trips to make on the mobile were easy in the house, especially with my pet Varmit. There were groups on at all hours of the day scattered all over and I hated to miss talking to any of them. I'd get up around five AM to catch the crowd around Wallace.

Seemed like Boss Man would go to the work twenty, crank up the coffee pot and start hollering for the group. There was Banjo Man, Thunder, Lightening, Warsaw Base, Honey Bee, Pump Man, Whip, Little Beaver, Little Beaver Squaw, Loud Mouth, Turkey Gobbler and anybody else that was around. All this saying "Good Morning" was taking place on channel eleven. It still wasn't crowded then. Now you can't get a word in edgewise. Wasn't long before we had to start using the other channels. Groups were beginning to monitor other ones and never went back to eleven. I had begun to monitor a channel with a group around Deep Run. We started using fifteen, but due to certain problems ended up on fourteen. Let's see, who were the originals. Night Hawk, Speed Queen, Monkey Wrench, Grandma, Wood Pecker, Crackerjack, Green Six and Hammer Head. What a group. Night Hawk drove an eighteen wheeler for TWT (Tidewater Transit) and had been on CB from the beginning. Back in the days of "White Faced Johnson's" and the like. He was the only one that seemed to know what was going on. He still gets my vote for the "MOST POLITE CB'ER." He was using a Browning Eagle then with that commanding "PING", D-104 of course, and maybe and little something else. Speed Queen, his XYL, was always around, listening, talking, really a joy to listen to. Monkey Wrench, now here's a prince of a man. Do anything in the world for you. Doesn't know the first thing about radios, key the mike, if it doesn't work, back to Freddy's, that's another story. Now give him a piece of farm equipment to repair, that's an entirely different story. He had already had several different rigs when I met him. He didn't like any of them. The Bengal base and Panther mobiles he had then just didn't do what he was looking for either. SSB and Monkey Wrenches just didn't fit in the same tank. His XYL, Grandma, is guite a CB'er too. Need anybody in the group, give Grandma a holler, she'll find them for you. Monkey Wrench kept a little something extra behind the seat in case he needed a little help making the trip. Green Six, how do I start? Here's a guy everybody likes. He just has an air about him that draws people. He's one of the few people that looks just like he sounds on the air. Most people look entirely different from what you'd expect. I used to try to figure what people looked like after talking to them, never was right. Six ran a Super Lynx, D-104 and Ground Plane. He also had a set of "Beams", well that's what he called them, two elements (or was it tubes?) whatever. He'd tell you to stand by while he put the beams on you. Then he'd blow you out of the room! Six had a voice just deep enough to drive that D-104 perfect. He had just built a den and it became his radio room. Everybody was always welcome to come by for cake and coffee plus a big helping of CB talk. Sometimes I wonder why "Miss Hazel" doesn't wring his neck, inviting everybody over the way he does. Hammerhead's the perfect CB'er. Never gets upset, always around, never tying up the channel. He used a Realistic Hoe & Shovel when I met him with a Starduster antenna. Operates a clean station, nothing illegal, just an excellent CB'er. Woodpecker is like me. Trying everything new, never staying with the same thing. Whatever's the loudest and strongest, that's what Woodpecker runs. Seems in the beginning, Woodpecker and Monkey Wrench made at least one trip a night to Freddy's in LaGrange. He operates the local CB Sales and repair shop. Has the best selections of gear anywhere around. He sure has the business, from the time he gets home from his regular job until, there is always a crowd around. More about Freddy later.

There of course are many, many others. One that always comes to mind is "The Square Peg in the Round Hole". Freddy Simpson would join the CB craze a little later. He would hold court late night and early mornings. That way he wasn't in everybody's TV. He'd keep you in stitches for hours.

He's an attorney, good friend of Daddy's and very special person to me. A couple of years before, I'd been asked to spend the night as a guest of Onslow County in Jacksonville. They were very insistant. Something about "Blowing 20 in the Breath-a-lizer"

What can I say, obviously a mistake. Freddy said he was sure of it. For the next 12 months, just like clockwork, I'd meet him in court. He'd look around, ask a few questions, then have my case continued. Something about not having the right Judge and prosecutor. On the twelfth trip. Everything was right. My case was brought before the Judge, the charges read. I'm sitting there waiting for the case to be continued….

"Stand up and say, Guilty your Honor."

What the hell was he saying. Okay I wasn't listening, But, Guilty? I stood up.

"Guilty, your Honor."

"$37.50 and court cost. Next case."

What had I pleaded guilty to? When we got outside, I asked. Freddy said the charges had been reduced to "Careless and Reckless Driving." I could have hugged his neck.

"How much I owe you?"

"Got a hundred dollars on you."

I sure did a hastily handed the twenties to him.

"Freddy, I can't thank you enough."

"Next time, there better not be a next time, it will be $1,000.00 at trip and I'll personally "Kick your Ass.""

It's 1999 and there hasn't been a next time. The Square Peg with the Round Hole isn't around anymore, but he'll always will be with me.

"Pipe Man, can you hear me now?"

Just above a whisper, normal tone of voice. My pet Varmit was just a singing. Let's see what they say now.

Traveling Man! Where are you?"

"Sittin in the home 20, taking it easy."

"You're 10-8 now, 10 over S-9."

"10-4, just checking, no more sitting in the car freezing to death."

"Hey Traveling Man, what have you done?"

"Store Man, I'm 10-8 and 10-10 now, got my base hooked up now."

"Teeeeeeeeen four, you're definitely 10-8. What didya get?"

"Cobra 139."

"10-4, she's blowing smoke, loud as Pipe Man now."

Thats what I wanted to hear, they'd been picking on me long enough.

"Break."

"Go break."

"Traveling Man, you in Richlands?"

"Negatory Good Buddy, sittin on the base in downtown Albertson. Who we got?"

"Mopar."

"10-4 Mopar, you sound different on the base."

Everybody did, clearer, louder, giving me fives, sevens, nines. Before I could barely hear them.

"Different! You oughta be on this end. Man you're blowing the pine trees down."

"Preciate that Mopar. Sure seems good not having to holler."

Wait till my Super Scanner came in. I'd really show them something then.

"Break, Break."

"Go Break."

"Traveling Man, you got a copy on Sneeky snake, Downtown "J" ville?"

"10-4 Sneeky Snake, Bring yourself on."

"10-4 Traveling Man, you're blowing smoke in downtown "J" ville, Whatcha running?"

"Cobra 139, Turner +3 and Cheap Ground Plane. 10-4?"

"10-4, sounds like you got a thousand pounds hooked to that thing. That cotton picker's loud!"

If they could see my face now, they would really call me all mouth. I was grinning from ear to ear.

"Forty roger Sneeky Snake. Preciate them good words."

Won't about to tell him about my pet Varmit purring like a kitten.

"How bout ya loud mouth."

Okay, Store Man started it.

"Go ahead rachet jaw."

"Rachet jaw? What did I do to deserve that?"

"Nothing motor mouth, go ahead."

"You keep that up and I'll go stick a pin in your coax."

"Bring yourself on, my little puppy's waiting for you. 10-4?"

"Crackerjack, that rascal got a dog?"

"10-4, a little one."

"What kinda little one?"

"German Shepherd, bout a hundred fifty pounds."

"Firgit it, I ain't going!! Hey loud mouth, you gonna listen to me?"

"Ten fir jaw jacker, go ahead."

"Fellers, listen to him. Pay him a little compliment and see what it gets ya. Traveling Man go to Channel Fifteen and see if you can raise the Texaco Man."

"10-4, Whats his twenty?"

"Capitol City."

"Raleigh! Cotton Picker, you know I can't make it to the Capital City."

"We have, if you can't, we'll just have to call you an alligator station. 10-4?"

Picking on me now, okay let's see who's alligator and who's 10-8.

"Break 1-5 break, hey Texaco Man, you got a copy on the Traveling Man, downtown Albertson?"

Nothing!

"How bout ya Texaco Man, come on back to this Traveling Man, downtown Albertson, Eastern North Carolina."

Dead quiet, ain't heard a sound. I could feel Store Man laughing.

"Go ahead for the Texaco Man, I got ya."

Damn, he was loud, bout blew my speaker out.

"Texaco Man, you got a copy on the Traveling Man, downtown Albertson?"

"10-4 Traveling Man, where's Albertson, Ain't never heard of it?"

"East of Goldsboro bout thirty miles, twenty miles south of Kinston. 10-4?"

"10-4 (Damn he kept getting louder.) Got my beams on you now. Blowing smoke in the Capitol city."

Blowing smoke hell! He was burning the woods down over here.

"Twenty over S-9."

"10-4 Texaco Man, preciate that. What am I putting on your meter?"

"Bout 3 pounds, sounds good. 10-4?"

"10-4, got some friends on the side. See if they can make it to the Capitol City. Give Store Man a holler."

Store Man?"

"10-4."

"How bout ya Store Man, got a copy on the Texaco Man?"

"10-4 Texaco Man, you're sounding good in downtown Beulaville, 10-4?"

Silence.

"Traveling Man, I can't hear him. Tell em to try it again."

"He's hearing you Texaco Man. (Ain't no way he could have helped it.) Try it again Store Man."

"How bout ya Tex….Squeeeeeeal M.. Squeeeeeeeeal N, Squeeeeeeeeeal."

"Cut that mike gain down Store Man. You're squealing all over the place."

Bobby must'a twisted the screw slam out'a the bottom of the D-104 Probably wiping out at least 3 channels on each side of fifteen.

"Did'ga hear him Texaco Man?"

"Negative, must not be getting out. 10-4?"

That tickled hell outta me. Grinning like a possum. He started it.

"Go ahead Pipe Man, give him a holler. You can make it with no sweat."

"10-4, Texaco Man, how you doing tonight?"

I had to back the volume down. He'd turned all the horses loose.

"10-4 Pipe Man, just fine, couldn't be better. What's wrong with that other guy? Blow his mess up?"

"Negative, his old weak mess just won't get out. Got some other fellers want to make the trip. Go ahead Cricket Man."

"How bout you Texaco Man. Got a copy on the Cricket Man?"

"Hey Cricket Man. You're sounding good. 10-4?"

"You're blowing smoke down here too Texaco Man, preciate it. Crackerjack, give em a holler."

Crackerjack made it barefooted. Weak, but he made it.

"Okay gentlemen, got to go. 73's have a goodun down east. Texaco Man, Capitol City clear."

"Hey Store Man, you still with us?"

"10-4"

"What's wrong with that weak hunk of junk?"

"I don't know. Cotton picker won't be weak long. 10-4?"

"10-4"

He wasn't joking either, wasn't long before he was really blowing smoke and cleaning the cob-webs out.

Still gotta find out more about those beams. Everybody I talked to with them were 10-8. They'd go from the ground plane to the beams and it was like turning a "Foot Locker" on. Must be something to them. Most of the fellows on Channel Fifteen early in the morning were using them. One guy would go from nothing to twenty over S-9 when he turned them in my direction. You could tell it wasn't a "Foot Locker" because as he brought the beams around the signal gradually rose. With them, the operator seemed to be able to talk everywhere. The Capitol City crowd would be in QSO with stations in Fayetteville, Beulaville, Kinston, Greenville, Tarboro, Wilson, Rocky Mount, Oxford, Henderson, Roxboro, Yanceyville, Reidsville, Greensboro, Winston Salem, Pittsboro,

Southern Pines and Sanford. Without "Beams it just wasn't possible. Its very aggravating to sit and listen to all those QSO's and not be able to hear 50% of them. All you'd hear was the operator. You wouldn't dare sign on in fear they'd try to get you to make the trip and then start on you about alligator station or, "You ain't got no EARS! To save face it was best sometimes just to listen.

"Hey guys, sorry, gotta go, someone's at the door."

Any excuse not to have to try and make that impossible trip you knew couldn't be done with your setup. When a station's home 20 is in the Capitol City and he's in QSO with a station in Wilmington and you 75 miles closer to the Port City and can't hear them, you keep your mouth shut. All the time you're promising yourself, "I'll get there someday."

Everybody said the real strong stations were in Greenville and Washington. They tell the story about one guy called the Hubcap I think. He shot five kilowatts through his antenna and it melted down the tower. Five KW's that's a lot more than some of the local AM and FM broadcast stations run. He musta knocked everybody else off the air for twenty miles around. It was really easy to tell who had the "Big 10-8 Stations". Just surf the channels and when you find one that's taking out 1, 2, 3 or more channels and either side of the one they were holding a QSO on. Thats a BIG ONE!!!! One of these days........Hell, I still don't have my Super Scanner. Okay, one of these days I'll be that loud. I was told the other day by a guy with a Super Scanner that it doesn't have a "flat side". I don't have the slightest idea what that means, but I guess one day I'll need it.

"SUGAR BEARS AND PINE TREES"

Early in March the Super Scanner finally arrived. I got home around four in the afternoon and there it was. Now here was the antenna's antenna. Naturally I had to put it together as soon as possible. I had to make sure it was all there you see. There couldn't have been more than a thousand pieces of it. "READ THE IN-STRUCTIONS FIRST." Big black letters on the front page of the booklet. Surely they won't talking to me. Let's see, assemble A, B and C first.

"This mess won't go together! Where do all these wires go?"

You see, a Super Scanner is a vertical beam with electronic switching or something like that. Anyway, red to red, orange to orange, white to white. Finally I got the three legged monster together. Now for the elements.

"Nobody said these things were eighteen feet long! What other surprises has this thing got?" The half with insulators go on top, non-insulated on the bottom. "DO NOT TIGHTEN THE SCREWS IN THE INSULATORS TOO TIGHT. IT WILL CRACK THE INSULATORS." Hell, anybody should know that.

Dear sir: Please send by return mail, one insulator, part number 333674, to replace the defective part shipped with my Super Scanner.

"Wait a minute!!!" "Honest, it cracked when I snugged it up. I put very little pressure on it with my 12" screwdriver."

It was holding good enough to try it out so I stuck it up on three sections of TV mast.

BE SURE TO CONNECT SWITCHING CABLE IN PROPER ORDER.

"What cable?"

It wasn't in the box with the rest of the stuff. NOTE, SWITCHING CABLE NOT INCLUDED WITH ANTENNA. God, another day shot to hell because of a lousy piece of wire. Back to Southeastern.

"Joe, I need some connecting cable for my new antenna."

"Okay, how many leads and how much?"

Questions, Questions, all I ever get is more questions.

"Hell Joe, I don't have a clue."

Of course I didn't have the presence of mind to bring the information with me. What do you take me for? I ain't no electronics man…..Not yet!

"Okay, what kind of antenna is it?"

Now that I knew.

"It's a Antenna Specialist Super Scanner."

Joe pulls a book down, looks up the necessary information.

"Okay, here it is. 4 leads and ground. How much you need?"

How much did I need? I hadn't given that any thought at all. Let's see the pine tree was at lest 80 feet tall and was about 30 feet from the back of the house.

"How's it come?"

"100 feet, 150 feet, 300 feet, 500 feet"

"150 feet"

"Do you have your coax?"

Coax!!! Oh God, here we go again......$$$$$$$$$$$$$$$.

"No I'll need that too."

"150 feet?"

"Yeah, that'll work."

"You need the Pl-259's and SO-239's too?"

"What?"

"The ends."

"Oh yeah, them too."

"Thank you very much, come back to see us soon.

And I would, again and again and again. Back at the home QTH, QTH? What the hell is that? Home twenty, that's better for now. After checking all the connections again and hooking up the cables, I stood her up. Back in the shack (that's what they call your radio room) I made the connections on the switching box and hooked up the coax.

This sure is a sexy looking machine with all the red lights and big indicator knob for switching to the different compass points or omi-directional (ground plane) mode. Now to see if it works. Considering that the bottom of the elements were only 10 feet above the ground it did fine. The north indicator worked great for Deep Run, Kinston and beyond. Southeast was Pink Hill, Beulaville, Richlands and Jacksonville. Southwest for Mount Olive, Goldsboro, Circle City and beyond. Now that I knew it worked, how do I get it in top of that pine tree?

"NEGATORY GOOD BUDDY, I DON'T CLIMB!!!"

Standing on a foot stool makes me dizzy. When I put the stand-off clamp on the edge of the house to hold the TV mast, it took two hands, two legs, and my navel wrapped around the ladder rung just to hold me up there.

Help! Who's going up the pine tree with my antenna? Sugar Bear to the rescue. Mike Foss works for the same company I do, traveling southeastern North Carolina. He'd been bitten by the bug before me. He was using a Midland 13-880 with a Siltronix VFO 90 for a base and CLR-2 in a pecan tree. Sure, there was something else. What he really wanted was a 12 tube Elkin. VFO? I don't have a clue, I ain't suppose to know nothing yet. Ask me later. Something about sliding between the channels. A lot of gibberish to me. When we were in town, we would meet for breakfast at King's and talk about any and everything. Victor King, one of the owner's was an avid CB'er. He ran Cobra's exclusively and loved them. He had bases and mobiles. When you saw him coming over, you knew he'd just bought something else to try. His base station antenna was a Super CLR-2 and he could really get out with that thing.

"Mike, my antenna came in. Who do we know that will put it in my pine tree."

"I climb trees all the time hunting, ain't no problem."

"When?"

"I'm not that busy Friday. Want to do it then?"

It was Wednesday, I wanted to do it NOW, but.

"Friday will work, I think I have everything."

With Mike Bow & Arrow hunting and in trees all the time, I felt comfortable having him tackle the job.

"WON'T FRIDAY EVER GET HERE!"

The bible teaches that the sun stood still. Guess what? It's doing it again. Thursday had been at least three days long.

"Bob, that damn thing's at least a hundred feet high. I ain't sure I can do this."

My heart fell out my shoes. Surely he wouldn't back out now. Walking around the tree he wondered how he was going to get to the first limb. I hadn't considered that. It was at least thirty feet off the ground. After several attempts, he got a rope over one of the limbs.

"What are you going to use to attach it to the tree?"

Attach it to the tree? I hadn't given that any thought at all.

"I don't know. What do you suggest?"

"As big as the trunk is, you're probably going to need a piece of angle iron with a couple pieces of chain bolted to it."

Out to Johnny Shepherd's in Pink Hill. After Mike explained to Johnny what we needed, he came up with a good looking bracket. He used a "U" shaped piece of steel with the chains. Looked like it would work fine. Out with the "Green Stamps" and back to the home twenty.

After looking at the antenna and all the tree limbs, it was decided to send the antenna up in pieces. Standing on the top of a borrowed extension ladder, Mike nailed some pieces of wood on the tree to haul himself up to the first limb. After what seems like hours, he reached the top.

"Bob, there's a bunch of limbs that will have to come down to mount the antenna."

After retrieving my 12" chain saw , I attached it to the rope he'd hauled up with him. Buzz, Buzz, Buzz went the saw. Down came the limbs. Big limbs! Up went the antenna bracket. Up went the tools. Friday was shot. Mike had been in the tree for six hours. Lunch? I sent it up on the rope. Took too long to climb up and down. Bathroom? What would you do? Yeah, yeah, we had a couple of light sprinkles on that very clear day. Del's customer's kept sticking their head's out the back door of the beauty shop trying figure out what was going on. They could see Mike in the tree when they turned into the driveway. The house sits about 250 feet off the highway.

"What time will you be here tomorrow?"

Tomorrow?"

Mike really had other plans for Saturday, but…..

"How's 8 AM sound?"

"Wonderful, I really do appreciate your help. See you in the morning. OH, do you need to use the bathroom?"

After six hours in the tree, there had been light sprinkles…….Okay, I won't go there.

Next morning at 4 AM. I could hardly wait. Listening around the channels Talking here and there, being very careful not to divulge me secret. Knowing I'm going to blow them all out of the water now. Finally after what seemed forever, Mike arrived.

We took the elements off and secured the antenna to a rope. After 20 minutes of climbing, Mike was ready to pull My Super Scanner up to it's commanding position.

"Damn Limbs!!!"

"Let it come down a little."

Pull it over to the right."

"NO!!!!! The other right."

"Okay, start pulling again."

"Hold it!!! She's hung again."

"Drop it about a foot!"

"Okay, try it again."

"HOLD IT! DAMN THING AIN'T GOING."

"Bob, I'm going to go back down to it and try bringing it back up with me."

"Think that will work?"

Climbing back down.

"Its worth a try. What we've been doing sure won't work."

"Hey, that might work."

Mike was staying one limb above the antenna guiding it up and I was keeping the rope tight. Limb by limb, hour by hour, we were making progress. I can't really appreciate what Mike was going through. I sure can guess though. Finally he had it in place. After attaching the elements, he was almost finished attaching it to the bracket when..........

"Mike, guess what? The coax and switching cable are still down here."

"God*#*;**%/#!=**@CH.........Moth.........*****%/%/##!!!!!!!!!"

Mike didn't need a rig. You could have heard him in Kinston.

The Beauty Shop door flew open, Del hollering.

"What wrong???"

"Nothing, go on back inside."

"What are we going to do wrong next?"

"I don't know Mike, we'll find something"

I attached both cables to the rope a he hauled them up. There was a lot of muttering going on up there. Glad I couldn't hear all of it. Now the wind began to pick up. Mike, the antenna and top of the tree were swaying back and forth. Doggedly he persisted. Finally it was in place and hooked tight. The wind was picking up more.

"Bob, go inside and check the standing wave."

"For what?"

"I don't wanna have to come back up here again to set it."

I rushed inside, made the connections, keyed the mike......1.1 to 1. Fantastic!!!!!!!! Let's see who I can find.

"Break 1-1, anybody around?"

Damn, forgot about Mike. He's still in the tree. Running back outside.

"Mike it's perfect! Come on down.

Seven hours after starting up the tree, Sugar Bear's feet were back on the ground. He was still mumbling something about never being that stupid again. Never would anybody get his butt in that tree again. (He did go back up two more times.)

"Mike, forgot to ask, did you point the arm with the orange paint north?"

"Bob, you didn't mention that."

Out came the binoculars.

"I can't tell whether it's red or orange, can you?"

"No way, let's hook it up and try it."

Naturally it wasn't but I worked that out. My North became Southwest, Southeast became Southwest, Southwest be.........Okay it worked. She certainly was one of the best investments I had made so far. It more that doubled my hearing ability. Even though I didn't understand it at the time it also cut way back on my interfering with other stations I wasn't trying to talk with. I was definitely 10-8 now. No more alligator station at the home 20!

"Breaker 1-1, Traveling Man, downtown Albertson, 10-8 and listening in."

"Break Traveling Man, you got a copy on Bill Bailey?"

"10-4 Bill Bailey, what's your twenty?"

"Turkey, down below Wallace. 10-4?"

Bill Bailey worked for the Electric Membership Corporation installing and repairing power lines. Later when I started selling CB equipment, he brought a box full of old glass insulators by, green and clear. I still have some of them.

"10-4, (I'd switched the indicator toward him. Brought him up 3 S-units) you're sounding good in Albertson."

"10-4 Traveling Man. Hey, what did you do? You came way up on my meter."

"Oh, I switched my Super Scanner toward you. 10-4?"

"I heard bout dem things, Good Buddy, you're blowing smoke in Turkey now."

"Preciate the good words Bill Bailey, just got her up in the pine tree."

"Breaker, Breaker."

"Go ahead Breaker."

"Hey Traveling Man, you got a copy on the Black Hawk in Goldsboro?"

I switched over his way.

"10-4 Black Hawk, got a room full of ya."

"Traveling Man, you're blowing smoke in Goldsboro. I'm on my mobile out by the Base.

10-4?"

"That mobile is doing a fine job for you Black Hawk. You copy Bill Bailey in Turkey town?"

"Negatory Traveling Man, don't hear him at all. 10-4?"

"Bill Bailey, you copying Black Hawk?"

"10-4 Traveling Man. Just can."

"Break."

"Go Break."

"Traveling Man, you copy this Power Wagon in Goldsboro?"

"10-4 Power Wagon, you're doing your thing. Bout busted my meter. 10-4"

"10-4, this old mobile gets out once in a while. 10-4?"

Mobile??? Damn!!!

"Power Wagon, that mobile's blowing smoke. You copying Bill Bailey in Turkey?"

"No way Traveling Man. Ain't got enough ears. 10-4?"

I knew exactly what he meant. Getting out on the mobile was one thing. Getting back was another ball game.

"Okay, let me get outta here. I've tied up the call channel long enough. 73's, Traveling Man clear."

I 10-27ed around to see who else was on. Ran across Varona Base talking to Boot Hill in "J" ville. I listened for a while a then broke in.

"Break Varona Base."

"Go ahead for Varona Base."

"Varona Base, this is Traveling Man in Albertson town, bout twenty miles south of "K" town. You copying me all right?"

"10-4 Traveling Man. Got a good copy on you. Ain't never heard of Albertson though. Say you're south of Kinston?"

"10-4, bout twenty miles."

"Tell you one thing. You got that thing wound up ;if you're that far off. Cotton picker's putting eight on my meter."

He was putting four on mine and sounding some kinda good.

"Break Traveling Man, come on back here to this Boot Hill."

I was barely hearing Boot Hill before, now he was ripping the needle out of my mess.

"Come in the house Boot Hill, what do you like in your coffee?"

"Take it black. How come I ain't never heard you before. Anything loud as you ain't no problem to hear. 10-4?"

"10-4 Boot Hill, just got me mess on the air this afternoon."

"Well, you got her right. She's doing it to it in "J"'ville. Whatcha running?"

"139 Cobra, Turner +3 and s Super Scanner bout eighty feet up in a pine tree."

"You running something else too. Too loud to be barefooted. You loud as I've heard."

"Well maybe just a little bit of help might be laying around. You ain't exactly no cripple yourself. What did you do while ago? I could barely hear you. Now you're filling the room up."

"I put my Moon Four on ya. 10-4?"

I didn't have a clue what a Moon Four was. I sure would later.

"10-4, she's doing her thing"

"Break."

"Go break, Boot Hill got ya."

"Boot Hill, you copying the Fountaintown Boy?"

"10-4, Fountaintown Boy. Howya doing tonight?"

It was night!! What happened to the sun?

"10-8, that Traveling Man's tough. Bout to blow my mess up."

"Roger, he's 10-8 all right. Give him a holler."

"I ain't got nothing to git back to him with."

"You're making the trip Fountaintown Boy. Bring yourself on."

"Roger four Traveling Man, didn't think I could make it. Hadn't got my mess right yet. 10-4?"

"You're making it all right. Not blowing the speakers out like Boot Hill, but you ain't got no problems."

"Preciate it, Boot Hill, ya'll carry on, just wanted to say hello."

"You better speak to Varona Base or he'll be madder than a snake."

"Oh, is he in here? How bout ya Varona Base?"

"Just fine, gittin hungry though, ain't had no supper?"

"10-4, okay, we'll let you go. Have a good night. 73's"

"Good night all, Fountaintown Boy clear."

"Nite Fountaintown Boy, 73's Boot Hill and Varona Base. I'll give you the channel back. Just wanted to check my antenna out. Traveling Man clear."

"73's Traveling Man, you ain't got no problem with your antenna, she's doing her thing."

Down on Channel Four, Pipe Man was talking to someone called Governor. He was north of Burgaw on Hwy. 55.

"Break Pipe Man."

"Go ahead Traveling Man. You blew my pipe off the table."

"Evening Pipeman. I finally got my Super Scanner up."

"Yeah, I can tell. How does that thing work Traveling Man?"

"Its got three elements on it Pipe Man. It switches electronically. All you got to do is find out where the person's at and point it in their direction. It points all your power into one third part of the circle. It also helps cut off the other two thirds making it easier to block out something you don't want to hear. When you ain't talking to somebody, you just leave all the lights on and it acts like a ground plane. 10-4?"

"10-4, switch it around."

"Okay, it's now on all three lights."

"10-4, you're seven on my meter."

"Okay, it's now pointed north."

"10-4, now you're four."

"Okay, it's now pointed southwest."

"Roger, now you're five."

"Okay, now it's aimed right at you."

"10-foooooor! You're pegging the needle. That thing does work."

"Break Traveling Man."

"Go ahead."

"You got the Governor in Burgaw. That Super Scanner makes a big difference. What's your twenty?"

"South of Kinston, Albertson."

"That cotton picker is blowing smoke. I thought you were around Wallace or Chinquapin."

"Negative Governor, I'm about fifteen miles west of Beulaville."

Governor was running one of those Eagles with the "Ping". Never had to ask about those rigs. That "Ping" told you all you wanted to know. Eight hundred green stamps for a radio. Some people had money to burn, Ha, just listen to who's talking. Certainly it was a beautiful radio, But…eight hundred bucks would buy a radio, box and beams. Its sorta like owning a Cadillac. If you got the stamps, drive it. Otherwise get a Chevrolet. If you gotta ask "How Much?" you can't afford it.

"10-4, I'm going to have to do something about my antenna. It's not hearing as well as it should. Maybe I should get a Super Scanner."

"Its doing it's thing for me Governor. Think you'd like it."

"Okay, Pipe Man, Traveling Man, I gotta pull outta here. Ya'll have a good one. Governor clear."

"73's Governor, catch you later. Traveling Man, how'd you get that thing in the pine tree?"

"Buddy of mine from Grifton."

"Does he do much of that?"

"NEGATIVE! Says it's his first and last time. Took us two days. You can bet he's something special in my eyes. If you ever hear Sugar Bear, give him a holler."

"10-4, I thought it would be a rough one. Reckon I'll have to stick with my CLR-2."

"Breaker."

"Go ahead Super B."

"Evening Pipe Man, who we got on the other end?"

"He's the Traveling Man, Super B, over near Crackerjack's. Give him a holler."

"Good evening Traveling Man. Don't think I've talked to you before."

"Negative Super B, I haven't been on long. 10-4?"

"10-4, my wife's from over your way. Nell Howard, you know her?"

Know her? I used to ride on the school bus with her. We dated once or twice. She's a beautiful young lady.

"10-4, went to school with her."

"How bout that. Small world isn't it. When did you graduate?"

"Fifty nine."

"10-4, she got out in sixty."

"Break."

"Go ahead Squirrel."

"4-10, who's on here "B"?"

"Lets see, Pipe Man, Traveling Man and I don't know who else."

"4-10, how you doing Pipe Man? Traveling Man, don't think I've had the pleasure."

"Roger Squirrel, hadn't been on long. I'm over near Crackerjack's. 10-4?"

"4-10, welcome to Charlie Brown. "B", ya'll coming over tonight?"

"10-4, leaving in a few minutes."

"4-10, okay, see you in a few. 73's, squirrel's gone."

The Super Scanner was worth waiting for. A little hard to get used to, but no real problem. The instant switching was worth a million dollars. Didn't have to wait for a rotor to swing a beam. Sometimes talking to a guy in Jacksonville, and one in Goldsboro at the same time would have been impossible without the Super Scanner. Handling a 10-5 was easy as pie .

"The Scorpion with the Big Sting"

It seemed as if the Kriss 300m's Crackerjack and I ordered would never come and I had to have something for the mobile. I'd seen those tube rigs the guys were using and was sure I didn't want one. I'd heard stories of how the lights would dim when that thing kicked in and about batteries going dead if it was left on. You could kill the battery in no time talking with the engine off.

"Kill a battery, me?"

Yeah, once. Didn't have anything to do with a CB though. I think I was 17 or 18. One Saturday night I was dating the police chief's daughter and we were parked on "Rabbit Hill" beside the Hillview café listening to the music. We were not paying a lot of attention to the time. I glanced at my watch and almost died. It was after mid-night. The radio had long since stopped playing…….well, we were busy. I turned the key……NOTHING! I tried it again, NOTHING. She was dead. Now picture yourself trying to explain to the chief of police what the hell you were doing with his daughter parked on "Rabbit Hill" after midnight. Yeah, Yeah, no more dates with her……. Besides all that, they had to be tuned. How are you going to do that with it hidden in the trunk. It had to be in the trunk. The Friendly Candy Company would see it if it wasn't. No, I had to have one of the new transistor types with the ears on it. Won't no reason to get out if you couldn't get back. Word was a fellow over near Goldsboro had them. Whip told me how to get to his place.

"Breaker 1-1, Crackerjack, you around?"

"10-4 Traveling Man."

"Wanta go to Goldsboro tonight?"

"10-4, what do we need to go to Goldsboro for?"

"Tell you later, let's leave about six thirty."

"Make it seven, see you then. 10-4?"

"10-4, Traveling Man clear.

It had to be up here somewhere. We'd already ridden by it three times, just couldn't see it.

"Whip said turn left on 581, go about three miles."

We finally decided it must be the Super Market (Rudy's) we kept passing. Sure enough, over in the corner, radios, antennas, everything. Linears? He had them. Beauties I'd never heard of. Elkins, Varmits, Scorpions, Bandits, Black Beauties, Black Cats, Phantoms, you name it, he had it. There was one I couldn't believe…A TWELVE TUBE "D & A", pre-amp and all. DAMN, that was a beautiful thing. He said she'd do a full gallon. God, a thousand watts! I sure could get out with that. BLEED ACROSS A THOUSAND CHANNELS TOO! Rudy said I could have it for $800.00. That settled my needing it. He didn't have terms like Sears. I told him I was looking for a transister type for my mobile. After looking at several, I decided on the "D and A" Scorpion II. It was a sexy thing. It even looked powerful in the cabinet with all the holes in it. Let's see, two switches, on-off, and BIL. Even had a green light to let you know when it was on. Really didn't need to, just holler for somebody. They'd tell you if it was on. One hundred eighty nine dollars, God, that's a lot of money, But, I needed it. I just had to get out on the mobile. We couldn't put it on that night, but you can bet I was home early the next afternoon.

Okay, Rudy said I had to use at least number 14 wire, where in the world? Oh, this drop cord will do fine. Clip, Clip, now I've got the wire. Out comes the seat. How in the world do you get the wire through the firewall? Here's a place beside the steering wheel. Hook it to the battery. Now came the problem. What to do with eighteen feet of coax from the antenna. I don't know why it's got to be at least eighteen feet. It's got something to do with one half wave lengths or something. Can't roll it up. Read somewhere that's a NO! NO! empty the trunk, 200 pounds of catalogs, golf clubs, Playboy and couple of bottles of whatever turns you on. Run the coax under the mat, then the jumper back to the front to the radio. Reload the trunk. Now that wasn't bad, Ha. Nobody but an absolute "CB NUT" would even consider all that work. Test time! I flipped the switch. The green light came on. Hey, it works. Try the bi-linear. The noise came way up. That's it, works like a charm. Nobody's gonna call me "Alligator" again. Back seat in, carpet down, hood closed, everything back in the trunk, trunk closed, yep, that's it.

"Breaker, breaker 1-1, anybody around?"

"Go ahead breaker, Junk Man got you."

"Junk Man, you got the Traveling Man, downtown Albertson. What's your twenty?"

"South of Pickle Town on 5-5."

"10-4, just trying out a new rig (You never admitted trying out a new "Bomb".) How's it sound?"

"You're about 5 pounds up my meter, modulation great."

"Preciate that good report Junk Man, this mobile oughta be right now. 10-4?"

"Traveling Man, if you're on a mobile, you got it right."

"Breaker."

Go ahead breaker."

"You're both 10-8 in Kenansville. Bout to blow this Rattlesnake's mess up."

"Howdy Rattlesnake, ain't heard you in a while. Whatcha up to?"

"Nuthin much, just sittin here listening to the "noise box". Traveling Man, how close are you to Deep Run?"

"Bout three miles Rattlesnake. 10-4?"

"10-4, got some relatives over that way, Monkey Wrench and Grandma. You know them?"

"That's a big 10-4. Talk to them every day."

"Tell em you talked to me. What channel they hang out on?"

"Fourteen, give them a holler tonight."

"10-4, probably can't make the trip. Ain't got much of an antenna. Ringo about ten feet above the trailer. 10-4?"

"You can make it Rattlesnake, you're sure making it here and I'm on the mobile."

"10-4, preciate them good words, see you tonight on fourteen. Ya'll carry on, I'm gone."

"73's Rattlesnake, til tonight."

"Don't worry bout that mobile, she's 10-8."

"73's Junk Man, thanks for the good words. Have a goodun. Traveling Man clear."

"Break Traveling Man."

"Go ahead Crackerjack."

"That thing must be working, I've got you on all the channels."

"10-4, she seems to be doing fine."

"10-4, ya'll coming over to play cards tonight? My new base rig came in and I want you to see it."

I wouldn't be playing any cards when there's a new rig to look at.

"Ten-en Four! Bout Seven?"

"10-4, see you then, KIR 1638 clear."

Except for five days, I never cut the Scorpion off until it died.

"GRASSHOPPERS AND TURKEYS

10-8 TOO"

"Now that's some radio!"

We got over to Crackerjack's around seven. The whole table was full of his new radio. It was twice as big as the 620. A Royce 1-640, three meters, clock and timer, switches and push buttons, she must have twenty knobs and buttons. Volume, on-off, squelch, RF gain, Delta tune, ANL, NB, Tone, AM, USB, LSB, AGC, HI, LO, Clarifier, SWR Cal, SWR read, Local, Distance, RF meter, Modulation, and SWR bridge. Then the clock, barrel type with timer. It had everything. Veneer wood cabinet, beautiful face with it's sexy green lights, made it look like a million dollars. Crackerjack had already put the Turner +3 on it. Didn't have to change a thing, wires, switches, plug, all worked. That was his kind of luck. If It had been me. There would have been another pound of solder, new plug, black tape…..although I must admit, I was getting pretty good with that soldering iron. Of course a special "Five pound package of my "VERY SPECIAL BLESSINGS" would make it work anyhow. Crackerjack's "horse shoes" came from a better store than mine when it came to luck. Somebody said that "You made your own luck." If that's the case, I've certainly been issued the wrong set of tools.

He gave several of the guys a holler just to show me how it worked. What a sound, lots of deep base. The 4 ½" speaker made a big difference. Frequency response was much better.

We were chewing the rag with Super Bee, when all of a sudden the needle went crazy. It was bouncing all over the place. The sound was crazy, part Super Bee, mostly mumbo jumbo. Crackerjack was mumbling something about damn Grasshopper.

"Crackerjack, what the hell's wrong with her."

"Grasshopper's got that funny radio on again. No telling where he's at, could be anywhere!"

"Funny Radio?"

I didn't know what he was talking about.

"It's one of those high powered rigs for ham's that's been fixed to work on CB. Got about a hundred watts coming out of it barefooted and they say it'll go anywhere."

Considering that CB radios ran 4 WATTS, that was a hellofa difference. God, that almost equaled the maximum 150 watts my pet Varmit could pump out.

"Go anywhere? What in the world are you talking about?"

Crackerjack didn't know much about it except it didn't have a channel selector with crystals like ours. Just one big knob that stopped anywhere. Of course neither of us had a clue about RC channels or channels above 23 or below 1. For all we knew, there were 23 channels and that's all there were.

Boy! It was tearing the radio all to pieces. We signed with the guys because of the bleed-over. Crackerjack flipped back to eleven and backed the volume down.

"Grasshopper lives up by the turkey houses just beyond Aunt Mag's."

that was maybe a mile and a half. He'd been hearing them (Grasshopper's brother talked on that thing too, called himself "Turkey".) ever since he got on. They'd tear his mess all to pieces every time they'd crank up. Looked as if we were really going to play cards tonight. That made the girls happy. First time in weeks we'd actually played. Lately, the Charlie Brown had gotten in the way. What were we playing? Spades or Bridge? The girls didn't care. They just wanted to play. After a couple of hours, the noise stopped. Then, all of a sudden......

"Grasshopper, 10-8, 10-10 and listening in."

I almost jumped out of my chair. He sounded as if he had just walked in the door. Never heard anything like it. So clear and loud, not too loud, the AGC took care of that. Crackerjack looked at Bo.

"Pepsi time."

What that really meant was we were going back to the radio.

"Breaker 1-1, Grasshopper, carry it to 1-3."

"10-4, Grasshopper 10-27."

"Grasshopper, this is Crackerjack, where were you for the past two hours?"

"Lower side band, fourteen and a half."

"10-4, couldn't find you. Just wondering."

"Mercy, been talking to Skipper (Skipper's home twenty was Pink Hill), cotton picker didn't know when to quit."

"Got a new rig with sideband, let's give it a try."

"Mercy 10-4, drop it down to the lower side right here."

Mickey Mouse and Donald Duck never sounded that bad. I'd never heard such sounds in my life. Crackerjack was twisting the Clarifier one way then the other. No way, we just couldn't pull him in. Back to "Ancient Mary".

"Grasshopper, I'm back on AM."

We waited for him to come back up.

"Hey Crackerjack, where'd you go?"

"Back up here, I couldn't find you."

"Mercy, let's try it again. This time don't move your Clarifier. Just count from 1 to 10 forward and backwards a few times. I'll find you. 10-4?"

"10-4, 1-2-3-4-5-6-7-8-9-10-9-8-7-6-5-4-3-2-1-2-3-4-5-6-7-8-9-10-9-8-7-6-5-4-3-2-1. How bout it Grasshopper?"

"10-4 Crackerjack, got you now."

He sounded just as good as on AM.

"Crackerjack, that rig sounds good on sideband. Whatcha running?"

"Royce 1-640."

"Mercy, cottonpicker's doing it's thing. I've seen pictures of them, good looking rig."

"10-4, preciate that. Grasshopper, I've got a friend here with me, tell him what you're running"

"Laughing, Mercy, it's just an old sideband rig. Siltronix 1011 Charlie."

That didn't mean beans to me.

"It goes all the way from 26,905 to 27,455." (Hadn't been converted yet. Afterwards it would go all the way into the 10 meter ham band.)

I looked at Crackerjack.

"What the world is he talking about?"

"I don't know. 10-4 Grasshopper, it's blowing smoke, tears my rig all to pieces everytime you come on the air. What kinda antenna you running?"

Now listen to this. Here's a guy with a seven hundred dollar rig.

"Crackerjack, its a CLR-2 or was, the radials broke off in a storm. Got a Moon Raker 4, just hadn't got it up yet."

"10-4."

"CQ, CQ, CQ!"

"What the hell is that? CQ, what does that mean?"

Crackerjack and I just looked at each other.

"Go ahead Skipper, mercy, I thought you had gone to bed."

"Hey fellows, who we got in here?"

"Mercy Skipper, I don't know. Crackerjack and somebody."

"Hey Crackerjack, I've heard you on AM, didn't know you were on sideband."

"10-4 Skipper, just got this rig. First time I've had it on sideband."

"Roger Crackerjack, you'll enjoy it. Talks three times as far without half the mess. (Sideband didn't require a carrier. That way instead of the 4 watts output on AM, your output would be 12 watts PEP. Yeah, Yeah, don't get technical.) You got a number to talk to the fellows yet?"

"What kinda number Skipper?"

"November Charlie's."

"Where do I get that?"

"Freddy's over in La Grange, he's out of them right now."

"10-4, I'll have to get one soon as they come in."

"Crackerjack, who else is in here?"

"Traveling Man's sitting here with me."

"He got sideband?"

I did, but I wasn't ready for that yet.

"Negative, not yet."

"Oughta get one, he'd like it."

"10-4, I'm sure he would."

"Hey Crackerjack, that rig got any sliding capabilities?"

"I don't know what you mean."

"Oh, can it talk between channels?"

"No, it won't do that."

"You gonna have to get a slider. Everybody gonna run off and leave you." (Yeah, Yeah, don't get technical.)

"10-4, I'm sure I'll have to."

"Get ya something like Grasshopper's. It'll go anywhere."

"10-4, I know."

"Hey Grasshopper, wanta go to Freddy's tomorrow night?"

"Mercy Skipper, I don't know if I can, depends on what time we finish feeding the Turkeys."

"Oh, that's right, well, let me know."

"10-4 Skipper, Mercy, this thing's getting hot. Better let her rest awhile."

"Okay grasshopper, 73's to you."

"You too Crackerjack and the other feller."

I found out later the reason I hadn't heard Grasshopper on before. That rig had blown up. Seemed to do it on a regular basis. Along with a screwed up antenna, the standing wave musta been in the clouds, he couldn't keep a screwdriver out of it. He and Skipper were sixteen or seventeen and spent half their time running back and forth to Freddy's. Each time they'd go, a new speed record would be set. Those back roads were just perfect for "low flying". Most of the time they'd be on Skipper's car, or should I say "un-guided missile". They were in constant touch with Turkey at home on the base.

"Turkey, we just crossed the bridge, coming up on 5-5."

"10-4, sounding good."

"Just crossed the intersection, hang on Grasshopper."

"Where ya'll now?"

"Just passed Liddell."

"Better watch that curve."

"10-4, Grasshopper's turning green."

You could hear Grasshopper laughing in the background. They'd be in and out of "Dead Man's Curve" just like it wasn't there. I never was sure if they ever stopped at the intersection in Albertson. They musta been running a hundred when they passed the Mormon Church. Then "Bingo", they'd be at Grasshopper's twenty. Twenty miles in fifteen minutes. I knew I'd never ride with either of them.

They came by the my home twenty shortly after hearing them the first time. Looked just like Mutt and Jeff. Grasshopper short and stout, Skipper tall and slender. I couldn't really tell what Skipper looked like under that long hair and beard. Sure turned out to be a nice guy though.

They talked about the kinds of rigs they wanted, Drakes, Swans, Yasu's, right over the top of my head. There was no way I could picture what they were talking about. VFO instead of channel selector, all the channels plus a bunch of other places to talk that won't legal. I still couldn't phantom what they were talking about. How in the world could you talk between channels, above and below them? As far as I was concerned, there couldn't be anything above twenty three or below one. That was all there was and nothing else could exist. It ended there. How could there be anything else? It would be quite a while before I understood anything about frequencies and their allotments. In fact, I had to see one of those funny radios first. It's so simple once you've seen one. One look at the dial and you know. Grasshopper said some of those rigs had five hundred watts in them. That was hard to believe. After all, mine barely had four. Swan 500 C's with 500 watts, that must really be something. They kept talking about other bands. Ten, fifteen, twenty, forty, seventy five and one sixty. They were Ham bands. All those rigs they were talking about were "Ham Rigs". Somebody had figured out how to put them on eleven meters. Hams used to have eleven meters til fifty eight. Grasshopper said the rigs had great ears on them too. Must have, good as he was hearing with almost no antenna. I found out later the "tube types" did have excellent "front ends". Much more sensitive than the solid states.

They talked about the "skip" that would be coming in during the summer. To someone new, it was hard to believe that when the "skip" was running, you could just as easily talk to someone in Canada and your next store neighbor. It was some months when the "skip" arrived that I really understood (or believed) what they were saying.

Skipper ran a Pearce Simpson Simba with a Siltronix VFO 90 slider on it. Actually gave him more places to talk than Grasshopper. Nobody in eastern Carolina knew how to convert the 1011 Charlie to UHF yet. He used a Palamar "Skipper 300" to compliment his setup. Of course the whole thing was in shop now. Skipper couldn't figure out why, it just gave up the ghost one night when he hooked the coaxes up backwards.

What was so aggravating about those two. They'd call each other on channel eleven and then go "upstairs". I knew they were talking but couldn't find them. My Super Scanner would reject the interference from Grasshopper so I could still talk, but that didn't keep me from wanting to hear what they were saying. Just like whispering in a crowd. They knew you were doing it but couldn't hear. Just like a private channel. Something everybody wanted, but few people knew how to come up with them. The repair shops knew how of course but they had to be careful. Converting CB's could get them in more trouble than they'd ever be able to get out of. It was being done of course, just being kept very quite. The most popular switch over was 22A. Some rigs just naturally had it. Turn the selector just right and there it was. On the older rigs that weren't synthesized, the operation was simple, just pop in two odd ball frequency crystals, bingo, you were there. The synthesized rigs were a lot different. If you knew how, clipping a diode, switching a wire or resister done the job. That was for technicians though. The easy way for 22A was switch two crystals. Take the one controlling channel one, two, three and four and switch it with the one for twenty one, twenty two and twenty three. Now you had 22A where channel three used to be. Of course you lost channel three. If the radio was traded without telling the new owner what had been done, it would drive him nuts. Changing any of the crystals to an odd ball one could carry the radio somewhere. The trick was to know which one to change and be sure the crystal was for the radio you were using. Otherwise you might end up outta this world in places God (and the Friendly Candy Company) didn't want you to go. Luckily, if you were too far, it would be out of tune it wouldn't oscillate. Some of the fellows around Kinston tried to make their own conversions. They didn't pay any attention to what they were doing or didn't understand what they were into. One rig used 23 MHZ and the other used 37MHZ. They couldn't understand why the same crystal wouldn't work in both rigs. Just like microphones, the 4 pin plug worked on most of the rigs, but the wiring was entirely different. Like me, they had a lot to learn. Time would take care of that. At this point, I was green, didn't know enough to be dangerous yet. If it didn't come on the rig, it didn't exist. Besides, I still enjoyed talking to anybody I could find. The channels won't tied up that much anyway. All that was in the future. Now finding a clear channel was no problem. The summer would take care of that. The big boom of "75" was about to happen. CB would never be the same again.

"Skipper clear and QRT."

"73's Skipper, see you tomorrow. 73's Crackerjack and Traveling Man, mercy, is that right? Grasshopper clear, QRT."

"73's Grasshopper and Skipper, KIR 1338 clear."

In the days, weeks and months to come, Crackerjack learned to hate that radio. Everytime it came on, he'd turn his off. There was no way to hear anything. His ground plane of course, didn't have any rejection. It was a long, long time before he tried SideBAnd again. He just didn't like it.

I think Crackerjack almost threw the biggest party of his life when he found out Grasshopper was going to another state to school. What he didn't know was that the radio would be staying home with Turkey.

"KBM 8355, INSURANCE MAN 10-8"

Joe Temple, to me was the "God Father" of CB around Eastern Carolina. He actually had sold insurance for many years, now certainly his first love was CB. Joe was in it from the beginning. When it became popular, he opened up a little shop as a sideline. He has probably introduced more people to CB than anyone I know. All you had to do was hear him on the air one time and you knew here was the "God Father". His voice, clarity, and Ping of his Browning Eagle dictated that. All Joe had to do was sign on.

"KBM 8355, 10-8 on 1-1."

"Breaker Insurance Man."

"Go ahead."

"Insurance Man, this is Yellow Dog, how's the rig sound?"

"Yellow Dog, you're 10-8, what's your 20?"

"Just north of Kinston, out by DuPont?"

"10-4, you're about 8 lbs. On my meter. Hope you're enjoying that new rig."

"10-4, wish I'd gone to see you sooner. Hey, you got any power mikes?"

"Brea…………..ker!"

"Go ahead break, KBM 8355."

"Hey Insurance Man, this is the Post Hole Digger, what's your twenty?"

"Home twenty, what's yours?"

"Out by Deep Run, member me? I got this rig from you last week."

"4-10, sure do Post Hole Digger. That Tomcat's sounding good. A power mike would help though."

"10-4 Insurance Man, I'll be by to see you soon as I can get my Green Stamps right. 10-4?"

"10-4 Post Hole Digger, 73's and God Bless You. Hey Yellow Dog, you still around?"

"10-4 Insurance Man, I'm still here, I'll be by to see you tonight. 10-4?"

"Roger Yellow Dog, see you tonight, 73's and God Bless You. KBM 8355 clear."

"Break Insurance Man, ye got base antennas?"

"10-4, sure do, what kind you looking for?"

"Don't know, whatcha got?"

"CLR-2's, Super CLR-2's, Super Mag's, Super Scanners's, Astro Plane's, Star Duster's, any kind you want."

"10-fir, what kinda Green Stamps?"

"I can't discuss that on the air. Come on over and I'll show them to you."

"Where you at?"

"Sandy Bottom, south of Kinston on fifty five. Look for my sign."

"10-4 Insurance Man, I'm rolling you way, Loud Talker clear."

"10-4 Loud Talker, be looking for you. 73's and God Bless You. KBM 8355 clear for awhile."

"Hey, Break Insurance Man before you go. Got any Boxes?"

"KBM 8355, you know I don't mess with anything illegal. Come by and I'll tell you where to get them. 10-4?"

He had them, BUT YOU CERTAINLY DIDN'T ADMIT THAT OVER THE AIR!!! Heaven forbid, the FRIENDY CANDY COMPANY would come take you away.

"Forty Roger Four Insurance Man, I'll see you soon. Lone Star clear and listening."

"73's Lone Star and God Bless You. KBM 8355 clear, I'm really gone this time."

"Break, Break Insurance Man!!"
Silence.
"Breaker, Breaker, Insurance Man!"
Silence.
That's the way it went day and night. Joe's eyes were bad and getting worse. He would sit in that recliner with cool wet towels over his eyes, place the D-104 in his lap and talk away. When somebody stopped by it was like old home week. He'd treat you like a long lost brother and talk about any and everything that came up. Sell you a CB? You bet! Joe's style of selling was "soft sell", the best kind. Before you knew it, you had radio, antenna, power mike, devices to stop that infernal engine noise, quick disconnects, maps, books, power supply for the house and a lesson on how to say "10-4". That part was free. The hooker to me was sitting you down in that recliner, putting that D-104 in you hot little hands and telling you to "have at it." There you sat, soft recliner, Cadillac of CB's (Browning Eagle), king of base station power mikes (TUG-8 D-104) and all the country at your feet. You'd bitten before you knew it. They just came by to look at the mobiles which they knew nothing about except that their neighbors had one and when they left, he had their mouthes watering for a $1000.00 worth of CB gear.

I didn't really get to eyeball Insurance Man until later, but that's another story I'll get around to.

"ME AND MY TRAM"

It had to happen. My Cobra was doing a great job, but I needed to step up in the world. I'd heard people talking about the old tube type rigs and how much better their ears were. Word was you could get better that 100 percent modulation out of them too. One night while I was channel hopping (10-27) around the dial, I ran across a real strong clear station. The guy sounded as if he was going to come in the room with me. So I hung around and listened. It was the Fifth Wheel from Pickle Town. That's about fifteen miles away. He was pegging the needle, but what was strange to me was even though he was loud, it didn't sound as if he was driving a freight train through the microphone. Naturally the guy he was talking to wanted to know what he was talking on. Fifth Wheel said it was an old Tram Titan Two, about seven years old. The mike was a UG8-D104, not the power type everybody used. Said it didn't need. It. That's for sure, it sounded beautiful just the way it was. God! That thing sounded great.

The next night I was talking to Whip and he just happened to mention the fact that a fellow over near Goldsboro had an old Tram he sure would love to have. Sheep Dog broke in and said the same thing. Boy, that Tram must be just the rig I was looking for. Road Hog over Wallace way came in. He'd seen on somewhere.

"Break Whip."

"Go ahead!"

"Whip, ya'll talking bout the old style Tram?"

"10-4, sure am, who this?"

"Road Hog, over Wallace town."

"10-4, didn't know, what you know about Trams?"

" Saw one at a jamboree somewhere, that's the biggest rig I've ever seen. Man swore you could get 12 lbs. outta it bare-footed. One I saw had a knob for receive and one for transmit kinda like the Eagle cept all in one cabinet. The receive knob didn't click and you could listen on the funny channels, say people talk on them now."

"Funny channels? Road Hog, what are you talking bout?"

"Place for funny people to talk Whip, you're already s'pose to be on them."

"Shut up Sheep Dog, go ahead Road Hog."

"Don't know much about them Whip, 'Sept there are spaces tween some channels called RC channels (RC stood for RADIO CONTROL, those frequencies were for hobbyists that flew the radio controlled scale model airplanes. Can you imagine what would happen, and did, when you were trying out that very ex-pensive model airplane you'd just spent hundreds of dollars and thousands of hours on and it just took off and left you never to be seen again.) and you can rig some radios to talk on them. Kinda like have a private line. 10-4?"

"Tennnnnnnnnnnnnnnnnnnnn....Fir! now that's just what I need so everybody can't hear what I'm saying."

"Whip ain't nobody in his cottonpicking right mind wanta lis-ten to you anyway."

"Sheep Dog, go crawl under the house and go to bed. Trav-eling Man, you still in there?"

"10-4 Whip, don't know what ya'll talking bout so I'm just listening, Roger?"

"Ten-en foe Traveling Man, I don't either."

"Hey Road Hog, whatcha running?"

"Cobra 135, D-104, CLR-2."

"What else?"

"Nothing Whip, don't everybody run power like you. You gotta 100 watts coming outta yer mouth barefooted."

"I'm going to act like k didn't hear that, Traveling Man, what you running?"

"You know what I'm running Whip, you're seen it."

"Laughing, Ten-en for'ra, okay I got to get outta here, Whip Clear."

"73's Whip, KJR-4734 clear, good nite all."

Seemed weird using call letters. Yes, they finally came, twenty one weeks after I had applied for them.

That settled it. I needed that Tram. I knew Whip must have been talking about the same rig I had just heard about, so I called Rudy.

"$400.00!!!! Damn, that's a lot for a used radio. Rudy don't let that thing go anywhere. I'll be up to look at it Saturday."

Crackerjack and I got up there about 5 PM. There she was, biggest radio I'd ever seen. What in the world were the handles for? Rudy said it was built to military specs. and they were for servicing. Already had the UG8-D104 on it. Must have good modulation.

"Okay, I've seen it. Say you'll take $400.00?"

Rudy said that's what he was asking but he didn't have it ready to go. What wasn't ready? Rudy said the finals and modulation tubes had to be replaced. God, that sounded like half the radio! Rudy laughed.

"No, just three tubes."

"Oh, that's different (I could do that)."

Rudy said it wouldn't take ten minutes. He just didn't have the tubes. Let's see (thinking to myself). I pick up the tubes in Goldsboro and be on the air tonight.

"Rudy, I'll give you $350.00 and get the tubes replaced myself."

"Okay, you got a deal."

"Sure"

"Crackerjack I got a deal this time, bet the tubes won't cost ten bucks."

"May I help you sir?"

"Yes, give me two 6GK6'es and one 12BY7."

70

A few minutes pass.

"Sir what kind of TV do these tubes fit it?"

"TV!, they go in a CB radio."

What kinda place was that Crackerjack? Radio Shack and no CB tubes.

May I help you?"

This was Sears, they had everything but, they didn't have them either.

"Bob, let's go by that CB place near LaGrange. He may have them."

"Okay, why not?"

Feeling a little desperate now.

"Ever been there?"

"No, but they say he's got everything."

"God Crackerjack, looks like somebody's dead."

There must have been twenty five cars in Freddy's yard.

"No Bob, looks like everybody's around that building in the back."

Probably having a party, but I needed the tubes. There was a party all right, thirty people waiting around to see Freddy.

"Hey Traveling Man, what are you doing up here?"

"Monkey Wrench, good to see you. Just came by to pick up some tubes."

"If anybody's got em Traveling Man, he has."

We waited two hours before we could get in the door, but time flew by. Get a bunch of CB'ers together and you got a real talkathon. Finally inside, still a few ahead of me, I just started looking around. He had things I'd never seen. Couple of things really caught my eye. Yaesu FL2000. That wasn't a radio, no place to plug in a mike. Fellow standing beside me said it was a two thousand watt linear. Took a hundred watts to drive it.

"2000 watts!! God, you could get out with that. Bet it would blow my antenna slam outta the tree."

"Yeah, take a special kind. Moon Four or Six probably."

"Probably would."

I didn't want to appear stupid, didn't know what the hell he was talking about.

"What's that thing over there?"

"There? Man, that's a Siltronix 1011 Charlie, how long you been CB'ing?"

Well, I blew it. This fellow knew I was a green horn now.

"Hey guy, I'm Freddy, don't believe I've had the pleasure."

"Traveling Man, over Albertson way."

He sure saved me from that frying pan.

"Oh yeah, I know some fellows over that way."

"Hey Freddy, treat him right. He's one of ours."

Monkey Wrench was looking after me.

"Freddy I need some tubes for my Tram."

"Okay, 6GK6'es and what else?"

"One 12BY7."

He didn't even blink an eye. Knew exactly what I needed.

"What else guy?"

"That will do me."

"Okay guy, $21.50, thanks a bunch. Come back to see me anytime I can help."

"Crackerjack, that guy's making a killing, but its easy to see why. Everybody respects him plus the fact he has what you need and can fix it when you break it."

A couple of hours later.........

"Freddy, when can I see you?"

"What's the problem Traveling Man?"

"those tubes I got from you tonight didn't do anything."

"Did the filaments light?"

I guess he meant did the tubes glow.

"Roger, but it won't get out."

"Traveling Man, bring it by Wednesday afternoon about six before the crowd gets here."

Well, another weekend shot. Just have to use that old Cobra till I can get the Tram going.

5:45 Wednesday afternoon, I was sitting in Freddy's yard when he got home from his regular job.

"Hi guy, be out shortly."…..

"Traveling Man, bring it in and let's take a look at her."

Cover off, checking here, there, on top, under the bottom, hooking up this thing, that thing, keying, adjusting this, that.

"Traveling Man, you didn't neutralize the tubes correctly."

Neutralize the tubes, what the hell was he talking about?

"You gotta check them closer."

He knew I didn't know what he was talking about.

"Grid current too high."

"Oh!"

"But, that's not what's the matter with her. This capacitor is bad."

Out comes the bad thing, in goes the good one. Key the mike, low whistle…

"Test 1-1-2-2-3-3-4-4-3-3-2-2-1-1."

"Okay Traveling Man, she's ready now."

Freddy handled that piece of equipment llike it was a thing of beauty. Maybe that's what drew people to him. Since then I've seen people there from two hundred miles away, eighteen wheelers from twice that far. He was like a magnet for CB'ers. It made no difference whether you were an AM'er or Sidebander's. He talked your talk and didn't try to set himself on a throne because of his knowledge and experience. We all lost a wonderful friend later, when he was killed in a hunting accident.

"Hey I'm wasting time. Got to get home and get this baby on the air. Thanks much Freddy."

Breaker 1-4, KHK 3958, KJR 4734."

"Go ahead Traveling Man KHK 3958 back."

"Evening Night Hawk. How's it going?"

"Can't complain, just sitting here resting. Getting ready to pull out for West Virginia in the morning. Rig sounds different, whatcha done to it?"

"Got another one. How's it sound?"

"Real good. No background noise, real clear."

"Break."

Green Six was joining in.

"Your nickel breaker, go ahead."

"Evening Night hawk, Traveling Man, you're blowing smoke tonight."

"Preciate that Six. Trying a new rig."

"Whatcha got?"

"Six, it's a Tram Titan Two."

"Never seen one. Who makes it?"

"Six, don't know. It's six or seven years old. One of the old tube types."

"Traveling Man, you got a good one. I've seen a few of them in my day."

"That sounds good Night Hawk. Maybe I didn't get stuck."
Break, KBM 8355."

"Go ahead Insurance man."

"Evening fellows, hope everybody's doing good. Traveling Man, Whatcha got?"

"Evening Insurance Man. It's a Tram Titan Two. Other than that I ain't real sure. Seems to talk and hear real good."

"It's blowing smoke in Sandy Bottom Traveling Man. Has it got any of the odd channels?"

"Insurance Man, I don't know. Just got it."

"Lets give it a try. Try 22A first.

"Okay, tell me how and we will."

"Turn the transmit knob up to channel 22, see if there's a click between 22 and 23. Then come back here."

"Okay Insurance Man there is an extra click up there. Now what?"

"Okay, let's go up and see if she'll talk. See you fellows in a few minutes."

"Okay Insurance Man, you got a copy?"

What's going on here? I can still hear Night Hawk talking.

"Break Insurance Man. You copy now?"

What the hell's going on? I still hear Night Hawk. Damn thing's already broken. One more time.

Break, Break, Break Insurance Ma............................"

A little voice from somewhere within….

"Turn the receive knob stupid."

There Joe was, hollering his heart out.

"Come on back Bob. I hear you. I hear you."

"Roger Insurance Man, just got to get used to this thing."

"Okay Bob, call me Joe up here. This channel's illegal."

"Oh! Okay."

"Let's see if you've got any more of them. See if there's a click between 23 and 1."

"Joe, there are two clicks beyond 23. Then you have to turn it all the way back to 1."

"Okay, go up to the first click."

"10-4."

"Bob, you copy me.?"

"Roger."

"Okay, go to the next one."

"Still copy?"

"10-4."

"Okay, let's see, that's 22A, 23A, 23B, Bob that's pretty good."

"10-4 Joe, still got some left on the receive knob. Don't know what's up there though."

"Okay, tell you what. I'll keep going up as far as I can go. Then I'll come back here. We'll see how far you can hear."

"10-4."

Bob, this is 23C. Going up. 23D, going up. 305, going up."

That was it. Far as she would go. I didn't know what the numbers meant. But 305 was it. Back to 23B. After a few minutes, Joe came back.

"Okay Bob, where'd you lose me?"

"At 305 Joe."

"Hey, that's good. I went up to 405 and stopped."

I didn't know then that meant ten more channels.

"That must be some rig you're talking on Joe."

"10-4, this is my pet. She's got a lot of extra stuff."

I found out later that extra stuff was an extra crystal box. He'd turn that Eagle to channel eight and go to another channel selector.

"Thanks Joe for showing me around up here. Guess we'd better get back down to 1-4."

"Okay Bob, remember, no call letters, 73."

"73's Joe."

Back down on fourteen, nothing but static. Too early for everybody to have gone to bed. TURN THE RECEIVER KNOB STUPID!!!! It was going to be hard getting used to this thing. Too many knobs.

I tuned around til midnight. Best set of ears I ever had or would have. I got all the way to Pender County that night. Little Abner, boy, now there was a character. He was a rural route mail carrier. CB certainly was his BIG love. Spent a lot of time on SSB. In fact, was the originator of the "Knot Hole Charlie" group. But, I'm getting ahead of myself.

One thing that Tram wouldn't do was talk on sideband. Bad filter or something. Didn't really matter. I wasn't for that yet.

SKIPLAND, SKIPLAND, SKIPLAND!!!"

Back in the winter of "74/75", there wasn't much of that stuff called skip. All I knew about it was what I'd heard other people saying about it. They kept talking about the summer months. According to them it would be impossible to talk to your buddies next door. Stations in California would come in stronger than anyone local. They told the wildest stories about skip. Nobody seemed to know why it came in. It just did. (It was all due to the solar flares and how intensive and frequent they were. This was tied to the 11 year sunspot cycle and Sunspot Cycle 21 was fast approaching. It's peak due in 1976. As the flares intensified, the "E" and "F" layers in our atmosphere were affected. The electrons were struck by the rays from the flares causing them to bounce around wildly. Kinda like the first time you were with that girl and your fingers accidentally rubbed across her breast, Damn right, I remember…..God! Where am I? Oh. When that happened, radio waves couldn't pass through and into outer space. They would bounce back to earth. Each time they bounced, that was referred to as a "Hop". The more intensive the flares, the better opportunity for "Multiple Hops". Stations being heard and worked in Canada, The Caribbean Islands, Middle and South America were being heard via " North/South and Transequaltorial Skip"). When it arrived, look out! We were all going to try and shoot those skipland contacts. The more power you had the better chance of getting through.

Spring finally arrived and with it, "SKIPLAND". Now Good Buddy, up until that time I had maintained my sanity, up to a point anyway. But then it happened.

"Helloooooo skipland, skipland, skipland. Come on back and talk to this Jungle Bunny in the flatlands of Kansas."

Now who did that lady think she was fooling. S-9 on my meter and I'm just pulling up in the yard. There she was again.

"Breaker, breaker, breaker 1-4, come on back to the Jungle Bunny in the flatlands of Kansas.

Well, I'd just break that lady and let her know she won't in no flatlands of Kansas.

"Afternoon Jungle Bunny. What's your real twenty?"

Nothing, silence.

"Jungle Bunny, come on back and talk to this Traveling Man downtown Pink Hill."

Still nothing, absolute silence. Hell, she didn't have to talk to..........

"Break Traveling Man."

"Go ahead Night Hawk."

"You're not going to talk skip like that. Get off the mobile and into the house."

"You mean she's really in Kansas!!!!!!!?"

"10-4"

"Hang on!!"

Now I was really tore up.

"Hey Night Hawk, you still there?"

"10-4"

"That Jungle Bunny was putting S-9 on my mobile!"

"Roger, that's the way skip works. Just listen, it's starting to come back."

There was the Unit 359 in Arkansas talking to somebody in Texas.

"Traveling Man, don't use your real handle or call letters shooting skip. 10-4?"

"10-4 Night Hawk, preciate it. See you later."

"Hey Broken Arrow, you got a copy on the Twenty Five Cent Piece in Eastern North Carolina?"

"10-4 Twenty Five Cent Piece. Come on back to this Broken Arrow."

"Man, you're blowing smoke in Eastern North Carolina."

"Hey Twenty Five Cent Piece, somebody dusted you britches that time. Try it again."

Opening the cabinet door, I checked the Varmit. Everything okay, Super Scanner set right.

"Roger, 10-4 Broken Arrow. Got a copy now?

Nothing.

"Hey Twenty Five Cent Piece. I got a copy on you. Come on back to this Dogwood Base in St. Louis town."

"10-4 Dogwood Base, you're blowing smoke in Eastern North Carolina. Bout 10 pounds

on my meter."

"Twenty Five Cent Piece, you dropped way down, but I can still hear you. Got an A-D? An A-D, what the hell was he talking about?

"Hey Dogwood Base, you're down in the noise, try it again."

I could barely him when he came back. Man, this skip was strange. Dead quiet again. Flipping through the channels, I found some more. Plow Boy was giving his address to somebody in South Carolina. I couldn't hear the South Carolina station. Plow Boy was saying something about he QSLed 100 percent. The gray matter was beginning to clear. A-D, Address, hey, that's it. They were going to confirm they talked.

"Hey Plow Boy, got a copy on this Twenty Five Cent Piece, downtown flatlands of Eastern North Carolina?"

"10-4 Twenty Five Cent Piece. You're walking tall in Indiana."

"10-4 Plow Boy (his signal wasn't fading at all.) You're wall to wall in Eastern North Carolina. Whatcha Running?"

"SBE Console Two, D104 and a set of beams up bout forty feet. What you running?"

"An old Tram Titan Two with a Super Scanner bout 80 feet up a pine tree."

"10-4, she's blowing smoke. You got an A-D?"

"Negative, not yet, but I copied yours. 10-4?"

I had lived in Albertson since I was eleven. Up to now, even though there were several mail carriers, there was only one route. No box numbers were used. There I stood in the post office trying to explain to the postmaster why I needed a box number. He was very understanding. In about 3 days there was a note in our mailbox stating that our box number was 213. Now I had an A-D!

"10-4, send me a card with your A-D and I'll send you mine along with some extras. Guess we'd better sign before the skip changes. 73's, 88's and 44's to the little ones. Hope to hear ya again soon. Plow Boy be clear after you."

10-4 Plow Boy, thanks for coming back. I'll get that card out today. Twenty Five Cent Piece, Eastern North Carolina, clear."

Listen to this, another breaker. Pocahauntas in Indiana, then the Powder Puff in Illinois, and the Eagle Claw in Minnesota. This skip was something else

That night all you could hear up and down the band was; "skip, skip, skip." Everybody was buzzing. Most like me, were new and loving every minute of it. The ones that had been around were saying how it used to be. Didn't need power back then, about how you had to run power now if you wanted to talk skip. You couldn't help it, If you didn't have a "bomb", they'd walk all over you. Night Hawk was telling them about the Twenty Five Cent Piece and how familiar he sounded. Everybody was getting a kick out of that. I got in and we ragged til midnight.

Next day it started coming in about 10 AM. I was up around Williamston, going over to call on the "Town and Country Restaurant when it started. I was monitoring channel 10 listening for smokey reports.

"Breaker 1-0, there's an unmarked wrapper (unmarked highway patrol car) on the overpass at the 130 mile post. Now friends, in Eastern Carolina, there ain't no overpasses, and there sure ain't no mile posts (big change between then and now). Somebody on Seventeen north must have thought there was.

"Breaker 1-0, what was that Smokey's twenty?"

I went back to him.

"Good buddy, I think that was skip. What's your twenty?"

"Just below Windsor, Southbound on 17."

"10-4, I just came through there. She was clean and green through the river field. Now Good Buddy, that river field, correctly called the Roanoke River Field was some stretch of road. I remember one time being carried through there on a Corvette well over a hundred miles an hour with a gal driving showing me how well she could handle it. last time I looked up the dotted white line was solid. Damn near scared the hell outta me. Last time I ever questioned a gal's ability to drive…. Put the hammer down, Traveling Man clear."

"Preciate that info good buddy. Have a good one. 73's, Green Machine southbound and down."

Inside the "Town & Country Restaurant" the family table was buzzing as usual. Several of the locals were there for their morning coffee break. Mr. Cortez Green, Mayor and local Ford Dealer (they say he really has enough money to burn "Wet Mules".), Mr. Gaylord Harrison, retired Dry Cleaner; "Doc" Taylor, retired farmer; Walter Parrish , Highway Patrolman assigned to that district, Mr.Dillon Cobb ("Daddy Dillon" to me. After my father died in 1979, he became more so and remains that way today. He and his wonderful wife Marie have looked out for me over a lot of years.), Restaurant manager and co-owner. He and W. T. "Teebo" Ross founded the Restaurant in the mid fifties. W. T. also operated the Ross Motel on the same property. It carried the "Quality Court" sign for many years and then the "Quality Inn" sign when the Logo's changed. They were also married to sisters. In the fifty's, sixties and seventies, Marie & Pearl worked as hostesses in the restaurant. H.P. Mobley, local insurance agent; and Chuck Sledge, Safety Inspector for Bitumous Insurance Company, He and partner Carl Baldridge "the Chinaman" traveled eastern North Carolina inspecting Logging Companies for Agencies such as Mr. Mobley's. Carl was one of my best drinking buddies. We'd start drinking about 5:30, eat about 7 and drink until one of us would drink the other under the table. Then Chuck would come over and help put the unfortunate one to bed. The T & C Lounge was some place. Yes, I'm a little bit prejudice. It was the first lounge I designed and furnished.

Chuck's been a CB nut for years, runs a Cobra 29 on the mobile. Goes by the handle, "Ally Oop", (Remember that song from 1960?). He really got a kick out of my first skip contacts.

"Bob, do ya'll really use those to keep up ;with us?"

"Walter, you know we wouldn't do anything like that..................Of course we do!!!!"

Chuck told him we knew where he was better than he did. It really was the truth. Up until now, the North Carolina Highway Patrol hadn't authorized the use of CB's on the Patrol Cars. A few of the guys had installed them on their own.

"Walter, those people out on Seventeen know you're in here having coffee. They know when you arrived and they'll know when you leave."

"I can't believe that."

Chuck told him to come to the outside, we'd show him.

"Breaker 1-0 for a smokey report."

"Go ahead Breaker. What's your twenty?"

"Northbound on 17 just south of Williamston, 10-4?"

"10-4, just came through there, ain't seen nothing cept one smokey 10-7 (stopped, not operating, off the air, etc.) at a local restaurant. She's green and clean, put the hammer down. The Lizard Leaper doing it thisa way."

Preciate tha info Lizard Leaper, I just got on 1-7 so I can't help you none. Ally Oop gonna be 10-10, 73's.

"73's Ally Oop, bring er on.

Back inside, Walter just shook his head.

"Gotta have one of those things."

Walter's Line Sergeant, Willie Rogers, (back in the fifties when I was a kid and Willie was a "Rookie", he was the Terror of Duplin County. We all knew about Patrolman Rogers and his super ability at keeping us from having any fun, well almost. One Saturday night we were all standing around at "Tiny Town" the local hang-out, talking about who's car was the fastest and as usual, that escalated to the point of having to race to prove the point. It was too early in the evening so 11PM was set and we'd meet at Woodland Methodist Church on the "Tram Road".

We all gathered about 11 and they started paring off deciding who would race who. All of a sudden flashlights started coming on all around us.

"DON'T MOVE, YOU'RE ALL UNDER ARREST!!"

Arrest, who the hell??????? There stood Willie Rogers, the sheriff's department, and God knows who all else. I was scared to death. Being only fifteen at the time, I was only an on-looker. They told us we were "Aiding and abetting". After a good talking to, most of us were let go and the key 4 or 5 were carried in and charged. Absolutely no "Pre-arranged racing for me." All mine was, " On the Spot" . Race now or forget it. I'll never forget the look on Willie's face when he said, " How old are you?" Never found out who the rat was. Guess it was better that way.) Walked in about that time.

"Good morning everyone, Bob, got anymore knives?"

"Morning Willie, No! Not for you."

Rachel brought his coffee over and refilled our cups.

The knife thing came from several years before. I'd shown Walter a sample of some of the knives I sold. (Let me fill you in a little on Walter. Story was that Walter was one of the toughest Highway Patrolmen on the force. He'd give his mother a ticket if she broke the law! We were about the same age. He'd been in the area for quite a while and really liked the people. He just wasn't getting any promotions. Between Jamesville and Plymouth, (before the bypass) there was a little "Bump in the Road" call Dardens. That was Walter's favorite hangout. When you passed through there,(it was posted 45 MPH) that's what you'd better be running. Otherwise, there was hell to pay and you'd end up in front of Bill Tetterton, a very special friend, one of the local Magistrates.

Walter didn't like to mix politics with his profession. After many, many talks and a lot of soul searching, he finally gave in and "Bamm", he was promoted. He was transferred once but managed to get back. He had been promoted to Line Sergeant before his return and one night on patrol just west of Bethel in a little area called Parmele, he stopped a car for a moving violation. The two thugs inside overpowered Walter and nearly killed him. He recovered and took medical retirement. Plays golf most days now and really enjoys life to its fullest. I should also thank him profusely for the two times he investigated my "one car accidents" and declared them unavoidable because the driver "went to sleep". Boy, he sure won't bad when it came to me.) Back to my story. He wanted one of the "Henckel" Boning Knives and I had promised him one. When I brought it to him, he was on vacation in Canada on a Goose hunting trip. Willie said he'd give it to him that weekend when he returned. Meanwhile, he had the Captain riding with him. He saw the knife, liked it and Willie gave it to him. Whatcha gonna do when the boss sees something and likes it, give it to him! Still chewing on his ever present cigar, Walter got into it with Willie about CB's and what he'd just heard. Willie told him the Patrol was aware of the situation and was trying to decide what to do about it. Several other states had already authorized them and he was sure they'd have them soon. Walter wanted it now.

"Bob, where can I get a cheap one?"

He was always trying to save a dollar.

"Walter, there ain't no such thing. They're selling like hot cakes. Nobody's got any cheap ones, but I'll be on the lookout for one."

Before I go any further, I've got to tell you about my first handle in Williamston. I was sitting in the T & C Lounge with Judge Tetterton, we'd become friends over the past few years. When I arrived in Williamston I met him and Bill Spivey at the

"Family Table" We knew immediately that we were Masonic Brothers. I was a poor excuse but still one all the same. They were both very active and had been "Through the Chairs" (held all the elected officer's positions) in the local "Blue Lodge". In fact, Bill had just come down "From the East" (the Master's position) being replaced by the then Chief of Police, John Swain. Bill Spivey was very active in the "Eastern Star and was "District Worthy Patron" at the time. That meant being gone many, many nights attending the various Lodges in the District. "Tet", as I called him was the local Magistrate and he and his lovely wife also ran a photographic studio in town. We became close when I had had too much to drink one night and volunteered to do a "Painting" for the local blue lodge. It was something they'd be using in one of the rituals and consisted of a piece of belt Weyhouser used in their pulp mill in Plymouth. It was about 8' wide and 30' long consisting of 3 sections. They'd been trying to find someone for several years to do the painting. There I was, too drunk to understand what I'd offered. They accepted. After that, I spent many nights on my knees and side painting that surface that was something akin to a very tight woven carpet. It had a very hard surface. This particular night I was nursing a "Bad, Bad toothache. It didn't matter how much aspirin or BC's I dissolved on the tooth, it didn't help. "Tet" listened to my bellyaching for awhile. Around 10:30 he suggested I go to the dentist. "Dentist", I hadn't been to one of those things since I mustered out of the service in 1960. That SOB damn near drilled every one of my teeth before I could get away from him. I made myself a promise that it would be a very cold day in Hell before another one got to me. At this point, little shivers of ice were beginning to form in Hell. After another 10 minutes and 2 more shots of "Jack Daniel's Green" I was ready.

"All right "Tet", give em a call."

"Bob, he said he'd meet us there."

When we arrived, "D" was already there. (he lived upstairs, after separating from his wife, that was the logical place.).

"Sit down here and l'll take a look. DAMN!!!!!!!!!!!!! "GAR-BAGE MOUTH".

GARBAGE MOUTH!! WHO THE HELL HE THINK HE WAS?

"Okay, Okay, pull the Damn Tooth."

"I don't pull teeth. I save them!"

He could tell right off that I won't at ease at all. He tried gas and numbed my whole mouth. After draining the abscess and giving me three shots of antibiotics, he let me up. The pain was gone or I guess it was.

"Okay Doc., how much I owe you?"

"Let's see. ONE THOUSAND DOLLARS OR…… Beginning next Monday, come see me each Monday thereafter until I get your mouth straighten out."

Needless to say, I took the latter. For the next 13 weeks, I was there every Monday. He couldn't save all my teeth. (My teeth won't bad. My problem was gums and bone loss.) I smoked 2 to 3 packs a day and up until then, did precious little to keep my mouth clean. I'm still seeing "D" about 4 times a year for maintenance and doing a fairly good job listening to his instructions. Hell, he's from Richlands, that's like being a neighbor.

As you can see……..."Garbage Mouth" was my first handle.

Back to my story.

I had one more call to make before lunch. Jo Ann Phelps was Food Service Director for Bertie County Schools. Jo Ann told me that her husband had gone CB crazy too. We talked about CB's for a while, finally got around to what she needed, a part for a steam kettle or something like that. I thanked her, jumped in the car and headed for the "Skip Machine." Seemed every mile brought another driver that couldn't drive faster than 40 MPH. I finally got through Washington and cooked 102 to Stokestown. Passing through Cox Crossroads, well you don't wanna know. Getting through Kinston was like being in reverse, home finally! I managed to get in a few contacts that afternoon before it fell out.

My first Canada, the Canadian Squeak in Ontario. Then the Trail boss in Michigan. The next one blew my mind.

"Breaker, Breaker Twenty Five Cent Piece. You copy the Polar Bear in Alaska?"

Alaska!!! Somebody was pulling my leg. Okay, I'd play his game.

"10-4 Polar Bear, come on in the house, you're blowing smoke in Eastern North Carolina. Bout 10 pounds on my meter. 10-4?"

"Roger Twenty Five Cent Piece. You're 10-8 up here in the cold country. What part of Eastern Carolina you from?"

Who is this turkey pulling my leg?

"Bout seventy-five miles East of the capitol city of Raleigh, thirty miles east of Goldsboro, home of Seymour Johnson AFB."

"10-4 good buddy, I was stationed there in sixty eight. Hey, got an A-D? I'll send you some wallpaper from the cold county."

Wallpaper? What the hell was he talking about now? This fellow was really trying to make an Ass outta me.

"Okay, Box 2-1-3, that's Box 2-1-3, Albertson, A-L-B-E-R-T-S-O-N, North Caro——lina, zipper 2-8-5-0-8, 2-8-5-0-8, 10-4?"

"10-4 Twenty Five Cent Piece, got her all, Box 213, Albertson, North Carolina , zipper, 28508, 10-4?"

"You got her all Polar Bear. (His signal hadn't dropped since we started. Who'd he think he was fooling?) Okay good buddy. Thanks for the call all the way from the cold country. Best of Luck, 73's. Twenty Five Cent Piece gotta go 10-7."

"73's Twenty Five Cent Piece. Catch you next time when the conditions are right. Polar Bear up in the cold country of Alaska clear."

"Hey Traveling Man, who were you talking to?"

"I dunno, some tinkerbell, said he was in Alaska."

"Didn't he call himself the Polar Bear?"

"10-4"

"Mind it I try em?"

"Negative, go right ahead."

"Break skipland break, Break. How bout ya Polar Bear. Got a copy on this Plow Boy, flatlands of Eastern North Carolina? Come on back."

Nothing.

"How bout ye Polar Bear? Come on back to this Carolina Plow Boy."

Absolutely nothing.

"Conditions musta changed Traveling Man. 10-4?"

"10-4 Plow Boy, who've I really got?"

"Termite, over Cabin way. Been listening to you a while. Reason I knew you were the

"Traveling Man. 10-4?"

"10-4 Termite, rig sounds good. Whatcha running?"

Now, there was one thing I was having to get used to with this skip. Usually when I was in QSO with a station, I'd always orientated the Super Scanner in their direction. Termite was due east of me. To favor him, I'd be rejecting the weaker signals to the north, west and south. Gotta keep the door open you see. Might miss a long distant call.

"Midland with a Ground Plane. 10-4?"

"10-4, doing a good job for ya. Well, gotta go. Better luck next time. 73's Traveling Man clear."

"10-4 Traveling Man, see you later. Termite Clear."

That night the usual crowd was around 1-4. Of course, everybody was talking about the skip. Some of the newer ones hadn't made the trip yet, but you could bet they were going to. The old timers still insisted it would be easy to make it "bare footed". What they didn't realize was that the amount of CB'ers had changed drastically and the days of "Barefooted" skip were becoming endangered. The FCC license applications had already reached a hundred thousand a month. Best anybody could tell, that was about one third of the total number of CB's being sold. Even though the license fee had dropped from twenty dollars to four, some didn't want to go through the hassle of filling out the application. It was kinda hard to understand and unless some-body helped you. There wasn't anyway to understand the darn thing. That plus knowing you had to wait three and one half forevers for them to come. Lot's of times unless the dealer mentioned the fact, people would go for weeks, even months, not knowing a license was required. After operating that long without them, who cared? Even though it was plainly stated in the rules and regula-tions that the rig was not supposed to be operated without a li-cense nor, was it supposed to be used as a hobby or a toy. Every operator had read and fully understood, (Ha) the Rules. Even had a copy close by the radio. That's what they declared when they applied for their licenses. Citizen Band was rapidly becoming the most popular toy and hobby the world has ever seen. Do you remember in late 1975 and all of 1976, trying to find the rig you wanted or any rig for that matter. It was getting harder by the day to find anything related to CB. All the popular brands were being gobbled up just as fast as they could be manufactured. Cobra's in North Carolina were as scarce as "Hen's Teeth". Wanting one was a joke. That's when the "Unknown's" hit the market. Every-body was getting in on it. It got to the place, if it had the letters "CB" on it, it would sell. Nobody asked "How Much"? Just get them a CB. CB's rapidly replaced tape player's as the Insurance Company's nightmare.

"Hey Mister, wanta buy a good CB?"

"No way!!! What kind is it?"

"Cobra, the best."

"How much?"

"$50.00, cash."

Cobra's were selling for new around $175.00 to $275.00 then.

"Well………………………………"

"THE BEARDED MAN ON THE HAIRY BASE"

Somewhere along here I started growing a beard. I'd always wanted one, but never had an excuse. The Greenville Kawanis Club, University City, had begun to prepare for the Bicentennial Celebration of Greenville and our Country. Growing a beard was part of it. I'd had a mustache for years. Now I was going to get a chance at the beard. The contest lasted some months and you should have seen them. There were all sorts of sizes, shapes and colors. Some closely cropped, other long and straggly. My was somewhere in between. It had to look neat or I wouldn't wear it. It was completely uniform in color, the gray hairs would come later. Bunches of them. Les Garner won the contest. Les was one of the officer's. He also held offices in many other civic organizations. I must mention "The Pirates Club". East Carolina University has a great football team and the "Pirate's Club" supports them 1000%. Les is one of the "Founding Fathers" plus one of the biggest financial supporters. Quite a man, plus he's also very involved in the Masonic Blue Lodge, Scottish Rite and Sudan Temple Shriners. Busy huh? I called the home office and cleared it with Lacy Walters, our comptroller. My life as a bearded man was beginning.

"Breaker 1-4, the "Bearded Man on the Hairy Base, is 10-8."

Just felt like fooling around with the guys, see what they thought of the handle.

"Break Bearded Man."

"Go ahead."

"This is Green Six, you new on the channel?"

Six of course knew who I was, it was going to be one of those nights.

"Ten-Fer good buddy, jest got myself some ears. How'm I gettin to ya?"

"Oh Bearded Man, you're 10-8 on Lightard Knot Road, blowing smoke, wall to wall, tree top tall, 10-4?"

"10-fer, let me jest my squelch, see if that makes me louder. Ten fer?"

"Oh 10-4 Bearded Hairy, you came up least 2 db. 10-4?"

"Hey Fuzzy Hair, (Night Hawk was getting in on it now.) Turn the volume up. You'll really get out then. 10-4?"

"Mer-cy!!!!!! Cotton picker bout near blew me clean outta de room. She's walking the dog now ain't she? Ten-fer?"

"10-4 Fuzzy Face. (I could hear Speed Queen rolling in the floor!) Now keep it that way, and you'll really get out."

"Break Hairy Man."

"Ten-foor breaker, come on back here to this Hairy Fuzzy on the Bearded Base."

"You got the Monkey Wrench over near Deep Run. What's your twenty?"

I could Grandma in the background.

"That's Traveling Man."

"Lets see here good buddy, bout three fives, four ones and some change. Ten-fer?"

"Negative Bearded Face, I mean, where are you?"

"Oh, 10-fir Mr. Monkey Wrench. Where I'm is. Good Buddy, I'm high atop the ground floor of the downtown Albertson Hilton, just beyond 49th. And 3rd. Ave., Under the 12th. Street "EL". You know, where the statue of Sir Albert Albertson looks out over the trade center. Take the subway and come on over. Ten-fer?

Now you gotta understand. Albertson is just a tiny bit larger than a crossroads. A couple of stores, post office and a café. Maybe 20 people in downtown Albertson. I live 4 miles from there. My license location says that I'm 3 and ½ miles southwest of Pink Hill. Friend, that puts me slam in the middle of the Maxwell's Mill section of Harper-Southernland Presbyterian Church community. Now that's pretty close. Okay, on state road 1555.

"10-4, traffic looks too heavy tonight, but we'll get over your way soon. 10-4?"

"10-4 Mr. Monkey Wrench. Hey, Mr. Green Six. How'm I gettin to ya now? I jest put my ear phones on Ten-fer?"

"You're up two more db's Bearded Hairy, if them things was stereo, you could really get out."

"10-fer! Let me plug in the external speaker, how's she sound now?"

"10-4!!!! You're pegging the needle now."

That's the way it went. Everybody just having a good time. For the first time since TV, neighbors were talking to each other. The handle "Bearded Man" stuck. Of course I use it on skip too. In fact, I must have used at least twenty handles talking skip. Whatever came up, I used. "Country Cousin" was the one I really liked and I ended up sticking with it completely.

That wallpaper did arrive from Alaska, you can imagine what that did to me. Now I had to have some "wallpaper" to exchange with all those fine CB'ers out there in skipland. Of course, I didn't have the slightest idea where to get any from. Most of the cards had some type of address on them, but not enough to trace to the printer. Most of the cards that looked professional came from CBC Club in Lexington, North Carolina. I began to ask around. Some of the locals had already checked the local print shops. The prices for "one color cards" seemed awful high. In fact, we found out later they were Damn High. Six had written to CBC Club requesting information. The catalog they sent answered all our questions. The instructions stated: Pick one of ours or design your own. I'll do just that. I had taken some 'drafting and was pretty good in art. The card had to be something special, had to catch people's eyes. "Bearded Man on the Hairy Base", that would be the subject of my card. Bearded Man, mountaineer type, bare to the waist, bald, (God, that premonition has haunted the hell out of me. I had a full head of wavy hair then and just a very few years later when Del and I decided to add a very large addition on to our home, Damn near all my hair fell out. I'll never build or add on to another nothing. Now I'm just another "Rogaine" almost has hair type) of course it goes without saying, pot bellied too.

Sure, just look down, beard down to the navel. Lets see, patched jeans, ragged bottoms held up with a piece of rope. Hey, looking good!!. Gotta be holding a D104, yeah, yeah, I know, it looks better if the TUG8 base is there too. Hell, nobody says all that. It's simply "D104". Radio sitting on a desk, AC cord plugged into the "K" in my call letters. That takes care of the bearded man. Address?, okay, Bearded Man on the Hairy Base, okay, what else? Oh, I was using "Country Cousin" for skip too. Had to put that somewhere. Still lacked something, why of course, my trademark; " May the Good Lord smile down on you and yours from the Big Base Station in the sky". I couldn't leave that off. Be like walking out of the house in the morning with no pants on. I tried to sign with it everytime time. Now when the skip was running hot, You were lucky to say anything at closing cause somebody would be walking all over you. The call letters were done in "Old English" , Big Mistake! If you didn't know what they were, you wouldn't. I used blocks for the different pieces of information. Each one a different color with a separate color for the border. The border around the entire card was supposed to be red. (It came back white. Hell, you can't have everything, besides I couldn't wait until I got corrected one. I used a magic marker.) All finished? Okay, ten dollars with the order, balance C.O.D. on delivery. Nothing to do but sit back and wait.

"Break skipland break, the Bearded Man, downtown flatlands of Eastern North Carolina calling, Bre...........................ak, Break, Ba.....................rake. Come on back and talk to the Bearded Man, downtown flatlands of Eastern North Carolina. I'm 10-8, 10-10 and listening in. Come on back to this Bearded Man."

I had learned the longer you held hey key down, the better chance you had getting through the Hetrodyne.

"Hey Bearded Man, got a copy on the Yankee Control, Land of Lincoln?"

"10-4 Yankee Control, got a room full of you. Come on back."

"10-4, you 10-8 in the Land of Lincoln. How' the weather down in Carolina?"

"Hot, Yankee Control, Just like summertime. Ain't had no rain in a month. How's it up your way?"

"Bout the same. Hey whatcha running? You're really blowing smoke."

"Stand by Cowboy, get right to ya."

He was about to wipe out Yankee Control.

"Tram Titan Two, D104 and Super Scanner."

"10-4, sounds great, I'm running a Johnson 250 with a Moon-Raker up about fifty feet."

"10-4, no wonder you coming down here so tall with that beam. 73's Yankee Control, got somebody on the side, catch you next time. Go ahead, Cowboy."

"Bearded Man, you're doing your thing up here in the Land of Lincoln. Got any Wallpaper?"

"Negatory Good Buddy, got some coming. 10-4?"

"10-4, how bout taking my A-D and sending me some when it comes in?"

"10-4, go ahead"

He kept getting wiped out, but I finally got it.

"Okay Cowboy, I'll send you some as soon as it arrives. Gotta get outta here, 73's May the Good Lord smile down on you and yours from the Big Base Station in the Sky. This Bearded Man 10-7."

The Hetrodyne was really pouring in. Worst I'd seen. Steady S-9. Sounded like a train coming through. I needed to do some work in the back yard anyway so I plugged in the external speaker (didn't want to miss anything.) and got to work. The next few days the skip just got better. It was lasting well into the night now.

That made local "Rag Chewing" almost impossible. The stations without a little something extra just didn't talk. Anything less than an S-8 or 9 got lost in the noise. Some folks just cut their mess off. Won't supposed to talk skip anyway. What they really meant was they didn't have anything to talk with. Talking on the mobile was out unless you wanted a Smokey report from Alabama or Arkansas. Anywhere but local.

April 29, 1975:

Skip was good that day. The noise was terrible. I got into Florida for the first time.

"Teakettle Lady on the Teakettle Base"

"Coffee Cup"

"Sword Fish"

April 30, 1975:

The noise eased off a little that day and the skip moved around toward Arkansas, Missouri and Tennessee.

"Mountain Boy Missouri"

"Wheeler Dealer Arkansas"

"Rock   Arkansas"

"Blue Baron   Missouri"

Then I got this one, "Little Fellow" in Tennessee. He was operating Daddy's base and I was his first skip contact. "Little Fellow" was operating barefooted and that didn't help the situation any. His signal kept going up and down into the noise. He kept insisting on giving me his A-D. I'd get parts, ask him if that was correct. He'd say no, and we'd start again. Since he was having no problem copying me, I finally gave him mine. He ended the saying.

"Bearded Man, please send me some "Wallpaper".

It was sometime before I heard from "Little Fellow".

"Hey, what's this?"

A letter from Bruceton, Tennessee. Phillip Smith, I didn't know anyone by that name. Yes I did, sure, "Little Fellow", Phillip told me about his plans for the upcoming summer, and about how his skip contacts were going. He wrote about the type of radio and antenna they had and about a set of beams that was in their near future. He also told me his age, eight years old. I wrote Phillip back thanking him for his letter and included a few of my new cards along with extras from the locals and all around the country. Sometime later I received a "hand drawn" QSL card from him.

May 1, 1975:

The skip was staying in about the same area. Noise wasn't too bad either.

"Blue Diamond	Arkansas"
"Swamp Boy	Louisiana"
"J. I.	Louisiana"
"SparkieEast	Texas"
"Unit 624	Mississippi"
"Widow	Louisiana"

May 2, 1975:

It started in about the same place. Then it moved around toward the Midwest.

"The 76	Florida"
"The 351	Louisiana"
"The 531	Louisiana"
"Six-Pack	Mississippi"
"151New	Orleans"
"Country Boy	Indiana"
"Angel	Indiana"
"Pawnbroker	Indiana"

Then it died down for a few days, or did I?

May 10, 1975:

"Tom Cat	Arkansas"

May 14, 1975:

"Double Duce	Indiana"
"Funky Phantom	Indiana"
"The 308	Indiana"
"The 244	Kansas"
"Beer Maker	Canada"
"The 387	St. Louis, Missouri"

"Night Stalker New York City"
"The 347 Wisconsin"
"The 319 Land of Lincoln"
"Iowa Corn Picker Iowa"
"Green Onion Iowa"
May 16, 1975:

It was picking up again, the contacts were better. They'd stay in longer, offering the chance to say more than hello, good bye.

"Dr. 13 Indiana"
"244 Kansas, again."
"Peter Rabbit Iowa"
"Carolina Transplant Missouri"
"Big Six Missouri"
"Spud Missouri"
"633Central Missouri"
May 18, 1975:

Back to the South. Good strong pattern.

"Model T Louisiana"
"Grave Digger Louisiana"
"238 Louisiana"
"133 Mississippi"
"Grasshopper Magnolia State"
"60-60 Louisiana"
"Rifleman Louisiana"
"Gator Man Louisiana"
May 21, 1975:

Starting to drop again.

"SkeeterOklahoma"
May 22,1975:

"218Michigan"
May 23, 1975:

"South Florida Farmboy Florida"
"South Georgia Mobile Georgia"
"Witch Doctor Georgia"
"The 2-5 Tennessee"
"Long Haired Hippie Tennessee"

"Glo Worn   Tennessee"
May 25,1975:
"Play Boy   Oklahoma"
"Grandpa   Rocking Chair Control, Louisiana"
"Boggy Man   Ozark Mountains, Arkansas"
May 26,1975:
The skip was all over everywhere.
"Angel......Venezuela, South America......South America!!!!!!!!!!!!!!!!!!

Oh yeah, I thought I'd done something. He musta been running 50,000 watts. I heard him every day for a month.
"351   Land of Lincoln"
"Outlaw Texas"
"Sammy Davis and Frauline Missouri"
May 27, 1975:
These were all good contacts. Talked with them a good while.
"Batman   Nova Scotia"
"Honey Bee   Nova Scotia"
"Big Daddy Nova Scotia"
"Polar Bear`   Saint George, Ontario, Canada"
May 28, 1975:
Another day of in and out.
"Flash   Mississippi"
"A-M   Columbia, South America"
"Computer Nova Scotia"
May 29, 1975:
Another all Canada Day.
"Big Blue Ontario"
"Happy Hermit Ontario"
"Globemaster Nova Scotia"
May 30, 1975:
Going crazy again, can't decide whether it wants to be in or out.
"Unit 64 Texas"
"Unit 95 Bermuda"

May 31, 1975:
Going to be a great day!
"Unit 308   Wisconsin"
"The 225   Wisconsin"
"The 776   Wisconsin"
"Seagul   lIllinois"
"243   Wisconsin"
I had been talking since four AM. I ran across this one at 5:50 AM

"Apache, What's your twenty now?"
Blackhawk was on the mobile.
"Down near the plant, be there in about five. How you copying me?"
"Apache, You're still strong."
They were both S-9 on my meter. They talked until Blackhawk arrived and signed.
"Break Apache"
Not too loud, just in a normal tone of voice. Don't blow it.
"Go ahead."
"Apache, this is Country Cousin. Hower you this fine morning?"
"Just fine, can't complain. Don't think I've hooked up with you before."
"No, don't believe you have. What's your twenty?"
He gave a street address in a subdivision just outside Dearborn, Michigan.
"What's your's?"
This was going to be good. Absolutely no fading of the signal yet.
"Albertson."
"Don't believe I know where that's at. What's it near?"
"Pink Hill, just south of Kinston."
Now he was a little bit shook.
"Country Cousin, where are you really at? Just down the block? You're pegging my needle!"
"Okay Apache, (Laughing), I'm in North Carolina."

"I've never heard skip like this. You're pulling my leg."

"Negative Apache, I'm really in North Carolina and if you'll take down my A-D, I'll send you some wallpaper."

I gave it to him, and returned his postcard a few days later. I sent one for Blackhawk to confirm hearing him on the mobile. (Hearing only, that's a WSL). This turned out to be the day with the most contacts on the AM side. I was back on the air at 6:30 after breakfast. It went like this.

"Night Hawk	Michigan"
"Gun Runner	Michigan"
"Big Man	Michigan"
"Blue Angel	Michigan"
"Super Fly	Michigan"
"187	Michigan"
"T-Bone	Illinois"
"Cry Baby	Illinois"
"Carpet Cleaner	New Brunswick, Canada"
"Annie Oakley	New Brunswick, Canada"
"Pretty Boy	New Brunswick, Canada"
"Sage	Maine"
"Stump Jumper	Maine"
"Globe Master	Nova Scotia" (second contact)
"Coal Miner	Nova Scotia"
"CCS 541	Canada"
"Digger	Canada"
"Organ Grinder	Ontario"
"Triple W	Michigan"
"Hawk Eye	Michigan"
"389	Michigan"
"Lucky 13	Michigan"
"Redneck	Southwest Missouri"
"8 Ball	Kansas

What a day. Never had another one like it on AM. I was elated and exhausted. The whole summer was like that. Skip every day. It was killing me and I loved every minute of it. Page after page of contacts. Looking back, I don't know how I survived. Up at 3AM every morning, when it broke, I was waiting. Didn't have to get Del up til six. Make coffee, back to the radio. I'd hit the road around eight, rushing to make my calls so I could get back home. If the skip was really hopping, I'd never make it to work. Sometimes I'd almost get to Greenville, Washington or Tarboro and it would start. Flip a coin, to work or "Skipland!" As you can tell, "Skipland" was a heavy favorite.

I should also inject in here that I was spending 2 or 3 nights some weeks out on the road. That part was really killing me. I was making contacts with my "souped up mobile' but nothing like the base. It was time for some changes.

"ANYBODY GOT A COPY ON THIS MOON SIX AT SEVENTY FIVE FEET?"

I'd heard so much about beams and was experiencing major problems being able to reject the "unwanted signals". It was time for a change. Talking with the locals, most of them were using "Quads" or 3 or 4 element beams. They were using Utility poles and trees to mount them on.

"Damn towers cost too much!"

How much was too much? I needed to get some answers. I went to see Freddy. He told me about how much each section of good freestanding tower was, problem was getting it installed. Freddy didn't install towers. He suggested I contact some of the "TV" appliance dealers. I drove over to Kinston and talked with Joe Butts at Southeastern. I had grown to trust Joe's opinions. He suggested I contact Don Brown at Brown Electronics' in Beulaville. I drove to Beulaville, found Don's business, went in, Don was out on a service call. Phil told me that Don did install towers and that he would give me a call.

Driving back home, my head was filled with different ideas about how the tower would look and what I would put on top of it. I knew it would take a minimum of 75 ft. of tower and another five ft. of mast to clear the pine tree that the Super Scanner was in. If I couldn't clear the pine, it would be a waste of time and money. The tree was west of the future tower location and would effectively block incoming signals. It was around 5:30 when the phone rang.

"Mr. Holt, this is Don Brown from Brown Electronics. Phil said you were interested in a tower."

"Don, call me Bob, in my profession, when people call you; "Mr", you know you're in "Deep Stuff". Yes, I want a Rohn Tower, about 75 ft. and I want it installed, turn key."

"Bob, I'll have to come look at your location before I can quote you."

"Fine, When?"

He could probably sense the urgency in my voice.

"How would tomorrow afternoon be?"

Now here's my kind of man.

"That would be great! What time?"

"Around 4?"

"That will work just fine. Let me give you some directions. Are you coming down the "Gun Barrel" or 111?"

"I'll come down 111."

"Okay, when you get to "Tiny Town", turn right and go about two miles. You'll pass Howard's Service Center and its the next left"

"Down by Maxwell's Mill?"

"That's the road", pass the mill and go to the next intersection. Turn right and go to the next house on the left. That's the place."

"Oh yeah, your father used to be the banker You live beside him."

"You got it."

"Now friend, time stood still." I tried every trick that night and the next day get time to pass. Finally, after what seemed several days, Don Arrived. He had that calming personality that I really needed. Looking over the situation and listening to my desires, he made a page full of notes and said he'd call me with a price tomorrow.

"Damn, another day to wait."

"Bob, Here's the package. It consists of:

Seven sections of Rohn 25G tower
one top section of Rohn 25G

one 20 foot section of mast
one 20 foot TV antenna
one base mount
one Ham two rotator
one Moon-Raker six antenna
200 ft of RG8 Coax
100 ft. of connecting cable for the rotator
2 ½ yards of concrete
400 ft. of Guy wire
4 each four foot anchors
Labor.

You notice that TV antenna? I ain't no fool. That was to get Miss Del's blessings. I told her she'd be able to watch "As the World Twirls" on at least 5 channels.

He gave the numbers in a lump sum.............My heart fell out of the other end!

"When can you do the work?"

"The tower sections and TV antenna are in Kinston The MoonRaker and rotator will have to be ordered. We can start on the tower Monday (it was Friday). By the time we're ready for it, the antenna should be here."

"What kinda terms?"

"Cash when I'm finished."

"Order it sir. I'll look for you on Monday."

"Mr. Luther" I need you!"

Luther Ledford is the local First Citizens Bank Manager. He's been good to me so far.

Monday, I was on the road extra early. I needed to call on Elizabeth City Schools and that was a three hour drive each way. I arrived at my destination around 8 AM. I followed Mrs. Winslow out to one of the schools, took some measurements for a piece of fabrication, then back in the car and back home by 2 PM. Don and Phil had already arrived and were finishing the hole where the base would be mounted. They had called the "Concrete Truck". I assured them that the truck could not get close to that end of the house. This was very sandy land. It could lay fallow for 20 years and you still couldn't drive on it. When we poured the foundation for the "double-wide", the truck was buried almost immediately. Took two wreckers to get it out. I volunteered to help with the wheel barrows. It really didn't take long at all. Sure looked like he knew what he was doing. Crackerjack and Chipmonk came over about the time when Don was finishing the concrete.

"Cous" looks like you're gonna be 10-8"

Don and Phil laughed.

"If this doesn't get him there, nothing will."

"How big is that antenna?"

Don went over to the truck and pulled out some information.

"Bob, looks like it's 32 feet long and the longest elements are 18 feet tip to tip."

He went on to talk about her other attributes: 16 db forward gain. Power Multiplication about 50X. Wind Survival, 90 MPH, Tuning; 26.5 - 30 Mhz., 12 elements; 6 vertical, 6 horizontal, Front back; 40 to 44, VSWR; 1.1 to 1, weight; 52 lbs. Well, I understood the 52 lbs. part. The picture was impressive. THE ANTENNA WAS MORE IMPRESSIVE!

"Okay Don, what time tomorrow will you start erecting the tower?"

"Whoa Bob, That concrete needs to cure 3 or 4 days."

"Damn Don, the skip will be gone by that time."

"Bob, trust me, it will be here longer than you want it to be."

I found out later that he knew what he was talking about. Being a "ham", he knew what was causing the skip. I didn't have a clue.

Crackerjack told me it was time to take a break. Why not play some cards? Come to think of it. How long had it been?

"Okay, or better yet, Let's cook out. Chipmonk and Miss Kitty (Crackerjack and Little Bo Peep's daughter and her husband) can join us."

Bo was on long weekend so that wasn't a problem and Del didn't operate the shop on Mondays. What to Cook? Seafood sounded good.

"Cousin, you go to Simmon's in Pink Hill and get the Shrimp and Oysters, I'll set up the cooker in the Egg Room."

"Got any juice? No, its been awhile, get us a fifth of Rare Antique."

Took about 20 minutes to get the food and return. Crackerjack and I mixed a good one. I began breading the oysters and shrimp. You always cook the shrimp first when the oil's the newest. We took another nip and put the first batch on. Crackerjack passed the bottle again. We had already reached the numb stage when everything was funny. When the first batch of shrimp came out of the cooker, we ate them and had another drink. If Chipmonk hadn't come down and checked on us, we'd probably gotten killed before the evening was over. As it was, it turned out to be a real nice evening. Crackerjack made sure the Rig was off so we could actually play cards.

The days drug by like going backwards. Finally on Thursday Don and Phil were back. The service truck and trailer were loaded with sections of tower. The first section was easy. They were on the ground. Now came the "Jib Boom". It was attached to the side of the tower and extended about 10 feet above the last section. They used it to pull the next section into place. Really, it went pretty fast. After about 5 hours, the tower was up.

"God, that's a pretty thing!"

"Yeah Bob, but we've just gotten started. The antenna was going to be the problem."

"When's it due?"

"Carolina Norfolk s'pose to deliver it tomorrow afternoon."

"You going to install it tomorrow?"

"No, it's going to take more than one day. I'd rather start on it Monday."

God! Another weekend without it. I didn't own a lot of patience back then. But, it surely had to come later.

"I half-heartedly searched around the channels on Saturday. I just really wasn't into it. Saturday was Del's big day so there wasn't much I could do but walk out the back door every fifteen minutes and check on the Tower.

Now, let's understand each other. As I've said before, I DON'T CLIMB! Walking around the base just made me want to climb up a couple of sections. I made it to the top of the roof, maybe fifteen feet.

"What the hell was I going to do if I needed to work on the antenna?"

I hadn't given that much thought. I sure would in the coming weeks. Hurricane season would really bring it to my attention. Right Now! Let's get this show on the road! After Church Sunday we rode over to Rose Hill to see Del's Mom and Dad. That really helped to kill the dragging time. Del's brothers were into CB too, but on a more level headed basis. They all had mobiles and it seemed to pacify all of them but Danny. He had a base station. We talked about the skip and how aggravating it was try to talk locally. They all used them to keep up with each other and the skip was hurting them.

We came back home about six, had a light supper (when you ate with Del's Mom, you didn't need to eat again the same day.) Watched some TV, I think I really read something about antennas I'd picked up at Southeastern Radio. Oh yes, I was beginning to get just enough knowledge to be dangerous. I've proved that many time since. Windi kept looking up at me. You could see it in her eyes. Why aren't you in the radio room? You're never in here. Get outta my chair! Later, when Randi came along. He'd be all over everything. He was much younger than Wendi. They both were crosses between Pekinese and Pugs. Both were black with a spot of white under their chin's. When Randi's mom gave birth. She chose our carport instead of her home next door Ray, Del's brother, his wife, Faye and the two kids, Kim the oldest and Tim had all made a place for her. (After Daddy died in 79, they moved into the Old Home Place next door.) She decided right at the last moment that our carport would be the place. She started having them about 8 that evening and delivered about every 15 minutes.

Guess who the "Mid-Wife" was? You got it. I'd pick each puppy up, dry it off and place it where the "milk machine" was. Randy was the last one and the runt. I couldn't detect any breathing at first and I gently pressed his chest area for several minutes. Finally he breathed. You're right, I had to have that one. A lot of years later, we had Wendi put to sleep. She had cancer and could no longer use her intestines. That's probably one of the hardest decisions Del ever had to make. She had wanted Wendi and I didn't. Wendi would remain hers. That day I held Wendi in my arms and walked all around the farm, telling her stories and reminding her of things she had done and we all had done together. When it was time, We put her in her bed and placed it in the van between the front seats. Very little was said on the way to Kinston, The Vet. was waiting for us. He administered the shot with both of us holding her. In a moment, she was gone. Placing her back in her bed in the van we brought her home. I buried her in the front yard in her bed with all her toys, and planted a Dogwood above her. It turned out to be one of the prettiest trees we had. Randi was never the same. He really enjoyed egging Wendi on. Bouncing up and down, running around like crazy, barking, barking, barking. When she was gone, he completely changed. It was as if he knew that he was no longer the kid anymore. He became Del's pride and joy and remained so until he passed away around 1996. She finally got another one, but I understand it sure ain't the same. Oh yeah, we parted in 1987. It had been a good marriage, but it was over.

I took Monday off so I could "supervise" the installation of my MoonRaker 6. As promised, they showed up about 9 AM. I could not believe all that stuff was going to be an antenna. I guess I kinda thought it would be partly assembled. Nothing was assembled. There were 24 pieces of tubing for the radials and they were in three pieces. The Boom was in 4 pieces. Nuts, bolts, screws, copper wire, fiberglass rods, stand-offs, mounting brackets. End caps. The list went on and on. Now I knew why Don said it would take two days. It took several hours to divide the parts into separate containers. They were trying to confirm that everything was there. The layout began with the assembly of the radials. They were all different. The reflectors had end sections of fiberglass to isolate the reflector wire from the rest of the yagi's. the driven elements were next to the reflector and the other four were parasitics. Each set becoming progressively shorter. The boom came in 2" and 1 ½ " pipe. The 1 ½ " pipe slid into the 2". That was all clamped together and the fiberglass rods (4 of them) were attached running along the length of the boom. They added structural integrity and rigidity to the boom. There was certainly a lot of pressure on them once the antenna was assembled. Now what to do with the boom to get it high enough off the ground to install the elements. They devised several X frames to accomplish that. The driven elements were installed first then the reflectors and then the rest. Lining all those members up and making sure everything was where it belonged took the balance of the day. I wouldn't appreciate until later why so much pains were being taken to get it right the first time. The setting of the driven element was especially important. Trying to reset it after it was in the air would be impossible. The instructions were very explicit about how that was done. They checked it several times. Tomorrow would be the day.

It was already late when they left and Del had supper on the table. We were just finishing when Monkey Wrench and Grandma drove up.

"Jest thought we'd come over and check on you. Hadn't heard you much in the past few days. Hot Damn! Cousin, what in the world is that?"

He hadn't seem the antenna, only the tower. I carried him around the end of the house and introduced him to the MoonRaker.

"Country Cousin, that the biggest damn thing I've ever seen. How in the world are you going to get it up that tower?"

"Not me Monkey Wrench, Brown Electronics."

Crackerjack drove up. Walking around the MoonRaker, he had the same questions.

"Be here tomorrow, they're going to put it up then. We all went in and the guys gathered in the "Shack" and the gals in the den. Monkey Wrench said he'd seen something like that MoonRaker up by a school south of Greenville on Hwy. 43. Thought that guy's handle was the "Hubcap". I'd make it my business to go by and look at that thing soon. (It was bigger, the biggest in the industry, the Laser 500.) I'd seen a couple of Moon 4's and some smaller ones like the PDL-2 Quad, but not the "Big one". We jawjacked back and forth about the skip, rigs, boxes, and operators in general. They all left about 9:30 and I went to bed. It had been a long day.

Don and Phil arrive early next morning. I'd just finished breakfast and walked outside.

"Today's the day!"

"Yeah Bob, today's the day. Lets get started."

He and Phil had devised a plan and they were ready to try it. It didn't work, back to the drawing board. They couldn't man handle that antenna. It was just too big. Next plan. Using the jib boom, they began raising it inches at the time. Phil was on the tower and Don on the pulley. They'd pull it up about a foot, tie it off, and get ready for the next foot. On the ground, there was no wind but up above 20 feet, there was just enough to create a problem. They lowered the boom just low enough to toss a light rope across the end of the boom. My job was to keep it from shifting around in the wind. That worked pretty well. Don and Phil took turns on the tower. They were gracious enough to offer me a turn, but I declined. Inch by inch, foot by foot, she began to climb. They tied it off at 50 feet and broke for lunch.

"Remind me to never quote an antenna installation again until I know what I'm doing. I'm used to FM verticals on business frequencies. I'd forgotten what this was like. Hell, my tri'bander ain't this big."

Tri'bander? What the hell was he talking about. I'd find out soon enough. Later, in my Ham career, I'd hang a TH6-DXX up there that would make this MoonRaker and his tri'bander look like toys. That's another story.

The afternoon temperature rose steadily. The hotter it got, the shorter the time one person could stay on the tower.

"Times a wasting, let's get this thing in place."

"Bob, sorry, you can't rush it. Climb up to where it's tied off. Try moving it around. You'll see why we can't rush."

Don knew I didn't climb. Hell, I was just in a hurry. We were drawing a crowd now. A few CB'ers and local folks wondering what the hell I was up to. From the highway it probably did look kinda strange. While they were resting I did walk out to the highway. It certainly was a weird looking sight. By the time I'd walked back, Crackerjack had arrived. He wondered if it was really possible to get it mounted.

"Just be patient boys. It just takes time. We'll get it there."

Phil went up next. You could tell he was tired. It was up about 70 feet then. They realized the Ham 2 rotator hadn't been installed. Tying the boom off, Phil called for the Rotator and mast. They wenched it up with the jib boom, mounted the rotator and inserted the mast into the top section. The mast stood out the top another 15 feet with 5 more in the top section of the tower. Phil came down and Don took his turn. They wenched that big baby up the last 5 feet and secured it to the mast with the attached mounting brackets. The mast won't nothing to sneeze at. It was a piece of top railing for "Chain-Link Fence". 1 ¼ ", double thickness.

She was finally in place. Fantastic!

"What do you mean, you gotta take it loose!"

"Bob, the boom's too long. We can't reach the connectors to attach the pieces of coax ."

"Damn, Damn, Damn!! What next!"

It was 6 PM and Friday. Don suggested we wind it up, they'd come back tomorrow and finish. You could tell they'd given it their all.

"Okay gentlemen, Tomorrow, I really appreciate what you're doing."

"Crackerjack, let's take a drink."

"Don't care if I do"

"Beer or Bourbon?" Let's try beer. Bout got in trouble last time with the Bourbon."

Del finished up in the Beauty Shop and asked what we were going to do for supper. I was considering drinking mine.

"Call Bo, see what she wants to do."

"She's working 4 to 12."

"Oh, cancel the call. You wanta eat with us?"

"No, Sandy's already got something on."

"Okay, let's have another beer before you go."

We grabbed a beer and walked back outside.

"What are you going to do if you have a problem with her?"

"Ya know L.C., I had the same thoughts yesterday." I don't know, but you can bet I'll be working on it."

"She's going to be something when its all hooked up."

I could hardly wait. Crackerjack left and I grabbed another beer. Daddy came over and made several observations about the new tower.

"What in the world are you going to do with that?" Thought you were already talking all over the country."

"Yeah."

It was hard to explain why I really needed it. After all, if you can't explain to someone that's driving a Ford Fairlane, how much better the ride would be in a Thunderbird......How could this be explained? He really knew a lot more about radio than I did. In his earlier days, he'd hang around Flavous Williamson's appliance shop. Flavous was always tinkering with Ham Radio's. He had one the earliest "Calls" around. Started with a X. In those days you built the rigs and Flavous was good at it. He kept the sloppiest shop I'd ever seen. If he ever made any money, you damn sure couldn't tell it looking at him or his shop. God, here I am talking bout kin people. His oldest son loves to tinker too. He was smart enough to have a "Guvment Job" to support his good habits. Ham Radio being just one of them. Boats were another. Reminds me of the time, Booty, his brother my age took Del and I along with his good looking wife Claudia on a fishing trip borrowing Pete's boat. like most of Pete's "stuff". It won't nowhere near new and was probably held together with hay bailing wire like everything else. We put in at just down from the bridge at Emerald Isle. Booty got the boat in the water with precious little help from me. I didn'tknow nothing about launching boats. I was much more interested in getting the coolers with the beer and sandwiches taken care of. We all boarded and he finally got the "inboard" started. It sounded like a broken sewing machine. No matter, we were on our way. Have you ever been through an inlet into the ocean? We hit just when the tide was coming back in. The water was choppy and rougher than hell. This was the last place in the world to have engine problems. We didn't have problems. IT JUST QUIT! The first set of waves took the windshield out of the cabin, the next ones came completely over it. Now folks, Miss Del don't swim. She started up my back like it was Jacob's Ladder, screaming something about we were all going to die. Die hell! All I needed was a drink. The engine finally caught and we made it through into the ocean. You didn't turn around in the inlet. Booty said that was poured in concrete. Didn't make any sense to me, but hey, what did I know? Out in the ocean it was dead calm with just a hint of swells. Everybody finally calmed down and the smell finally went away. Boots and I consumed several beers. Bout half a case, while Del and Claudia had sandwiches and Pepsi's. You know, to this day, I don't think Del's been even close to a boat.

Now Pete's retired and tinkers with this and that and really enjoys his hobbies.

"Yeah Daddy, it's hard to explain. I've reached this plateau and want to climb higher. That's about the best way I know to explain it."

He walked back across the yard to the house. He'd completely retired a couple of years earlier and just "pittled around the farm. His asthma was proving to be a real problem along with the emphysema. The "Chicken Houses" were built for him to retire, but his lungs just couldn't handle it. He'd sold the two chicken houses to Del's brother, Ray. He had converted them from "Broiler's to Layers" and was under contract to supply hatching eggs to hatcheries along Maryland's eastern shore and Del Marva Peninsula. The work was exhausting, and was 7 days a week. But, it paid good. Ray and Faye did real well with them until the "Snow of 80". The chicken houses caved in and were a complete loss. I really don't think Ray will ever recover from it. Financially maybe, but not mentally. He's never been the same.

I finally gave it up and walked back inside. Del was watching TV with Windi. I walked down to the Shack and tuned around the band, not a lot happening. I stopped on 1-4 just in time to hear Monkey Wrench trying to explain to Green Six just how big Cousin's Antenna was.

"Monkey Wrench, you know not. How's that thing going to stay in the air when a hurricane comes?

Now six, you didn't have to ask that. I didn't have an answer, but I was going to work on it.

"Cousin will do something. He always does. Six you gotta see that thing."

"10-4, When he gets it going, we'll go over and take a look. He been on tonight?"

"Ain't heard nothing from him. Bet he's worn out."

I was and stayed completely out of the QSO. I ran across some guys talking about SSB up on 22A. Acted as if they knew what they were talking about. Said there was a whole lot more activity on sideband during skip because the carrier wasn't in there driving you nuts. Now that made sense. No carrier, no Hetrodyne. Maybe I outta look into it. I think I've bit off about all I can chew right now. I shut down and went to bed. Tomorrow would be another day.

And another day it was. I stood in the front yard and watched the sun come up. It was going to be a beautiful day, hot, but beautiful. Wendi was out for her morning stroll, I walked her over by the tower. Del's day always started early on Saturday. She was walking out the door heading toward the Beauty Shop.

"Bobby, look after my baby. Put her back in the house before those people come."

"Yes Del."

I damn sure won't going to let nothing happen to her. She'd kill me and I knew it.

"All right Windi, let's go."

Absolutely stone deaf. Ain't heard nothing! Could hear a cat meow at a 1000 yards, but couldn't hear me.

"All right!, lets go."

Finally she ambled toward the door. Just in time too. Don and Phil were driving up. After being sure the she were safely in. I walked over to the truck.

"Morning Gentlemen"

God, they looked beat.

"Morning Bob, short night, had to go work on two TV's before I could call it a night."

Phil just grunted.

"I'm already tired."

Don was ready.

"Let's get this show on the road."

Getting the coax attached proved to be quite a job. The boom was so long, one of the "Flat" elements had to be removed to get the section close enough to reach the connectors.

"Okay, the connections are made!"

There was a look of relief on Don's face. After attaching the removed element, the boom was brought back to the proper position and secured.

"Hey! We're done!"

"Whoa Bob. We've still got a lot to do."

"Like what?"

"Rotator cable connections, Alignment, Guy wires. Remember your TV antenna. We've got to drop the mast to install the TV antenna."

Hell, I'd forgotten all about that. They tied off the boom and dropped the mast down. After installing the new Quantum 20' antenna, they ran it back up and into the top mount. That put the TV antenna at 90 feet. Del damn sure had TV reception now.

Phil was back on the tower now. He made the rotator connections and came down. Should they check the "Rotator" now and the VSWR or wait until the guy wires were installed? It was dead calm. One of those "Bermuda highs" was in control of the weather. There probably wouldn't be any wind all day. Running the two pieces of RG-8, RG-59, TV coax, and the cable wires under the house didn't take that long. They made the connections in the Shack and tried the Ham 2.

"Is it moving?"

"Yeah"

"Clockwise or Counter-clockwise?"

"Counter-clockwise."

That part was right.

"Okay, get the compass out of the truck and let's line her up."

Phil got the compass and stood at the base of the tower.

"it's pointing about 10 degrees west of due north."

Turning the indicator about 10 degrees clockwise.

"Okay, how bout that?"

Phil backed off, took a good look, came back, looked up again.

"Looks to be about 2 degrees east of north"

Don backed her off 2 degrees counter-clockwise.

"Now?"

"Perfect."

He calibrated and set it. Coming back outside.

"We're a lot closer than we were."

They unloaded the guy wires and anchors. Walking off fifty feet in four equal directions indicated the positions of each anchor. Screwing them into the soft ground wasn't difficult at all.

"Sure wish we'd had this kinda soil a couple of weeks ago up near Clayton. Trying to drive those anchors into the red clay was tough."

They'd already dropped the jib boom below the antenna and used it to haul up each piece of wire. Using a "Come-A-Long" they winched each guy wire taught.

"Hey Cousin, you're ready. Only one thing left."

"Yeah, what?"

I couldn't see anything left to do.

"Green Stamps"

"Oh yeah, come on in."

There was a lot of joy in writing that check. After a spell on the "Prayer Mat" in front of Mr. Luther's desk, he'd found a way to handle the loan. Said something about if he'd listed it as a loan for CB antennas and towers, the bank would probably dis-own him. He'd gotten involved in the craze too. Only from a mobile aspect though. He used them to talk back and forth on his numerous trips with the Boy Scouts. He was Scout Master of troop 244 sponsored by Pink Hill Methodist Church. Both his sons, Ellis and Tim became Eagle Scouts along with a great many more. I joined the troop in 79 as one of the many Assistant Scout Masters he had. Like everybody else the skip was creating problems for him. Later, I would rectify that with a special little box attached to the side of his rig. It sent him about 20 channels below one. He didn't know where he was so it didn't matter. It was quiet down there. They (3 of them) were listed in the directory as Government Channels. Hell, they won't using them.

I wrote Don a check and thanked him profusely. I would thank him many more times in the future. I walked him outside, thanked Phil and walked back into the Shack.

Don had installed an antenna switch giving me capabilities to switch back and forth between the Super Scanner and Moon 6. I moved the Tram up to 23C where it was sure to be quiet.

"Damn, sidebanders."

Sounded like a bunch of Monkeys fighting with their vocal cords tied in knots.

"Thats a strong signal. Wonder if its local or skip. I was on the MoonRaker and it was pointing west-northwest. I moved it about

5 degrees north. The modulation weakened. Moving it counter-clockwise brought the modulation up. It was strongest due west. I switched to the Super Scanner. Damn near lost them. I dropped down to 1-4. Pipeman was in QSO with Monkey Wrench. I was hearing both of them off the side and back of the beam. Pipeman was down in the dirt. Bringing the Raker east, he bout blew me outta the room. Monkey Wrench was on the side now and way down. I checked the cabinet to see if my Varmit was purring. She was ready and waiting. I wanted this loud and strong. I fiddled with the rotator just to be sure I was dead on him……….From way down deeeeeeeep.

"Break Pipe Man."

"Jeeeeesus Christ!!!!!" Cousin, are you in my front yard?"

"Negative Pipe Man. I'm at the home twenty. Evening Monkey Wrench"

"Evening Cousin, you're weak."

"He sure ain't weak over here! Cousin, you got dem beams up ain'tcha?"

"That's a big 10-4, Pipe Man."

"Swing that thing around some. Let's see what happens."

"Okay, here we go. Moving around toward Monkey Wrench. Okay, it's pointed at Monkey Wrench now."

"Cous, come on in, you just blew Grandma out the back door."

"Cousin, you dropped all the way down to a S-3. That's good."

"You're on the side now."

Swinging it around.

"I'm going to put you on the back. 10-4?"

"10-4, you're down in the dirt."

I could barely hear him now. Switching back to the Super Scanner,

"It's got good rejection, don't it?"

"10-4, did you put the Moon 6 up?"

"Roger, at about 80 ft, or Brown Electronics did. Don knows what he's doing."

"Pipe Man, me and Grandma went and seen it before it was up. Biggest antenna around here."

Yeah, this side of that Laser 500 across from Chicod School, it was.

"10-4, Cousin, shot any skip with it yet?"

"Negative, just got it on the air."

The channel rapidly filled up. All wanted to see how much the signal rose and fell with each rotation. All of a sudden it was 11PM. I'd ignored Del's repeated calls to supper. She had finally brought a tray and left it. I have no clue what she brought. You could easily say that I certainly had a "One Track Mind" that night. I shut the Shack down and almost made it to the bedroom.

"I gotta go out a check on my MoonRaker first."

There she stood in the moonlight. God, she was awesome. Visions of sugar plums rapidly turned into calls for the "Country Cousin" from all parts of the world.

The next weeks were happy ones. The Moon 6 proved to be just as good as advertised plus a whole lot more. Contacts were so much easier to hold and the unwanted clamor was way down from before. Of course when the Hetrodyne was up. That baby magnified it. I began to spend a lot more time on the odd channels and the contacts were becoming more technical. They seemed to be more interested in what you were running a what you had done to enhance your operation. I was eating that stuff up.

I filled page after page up with contacts. Here are just a few. You probably talked to them too.

June 25, 1975

"Double M Louisiana"

"AC 36	ILL."
"394	Miami, Fla."
"Triple 7	Nova Scotia"
"Unit 308	Kansas"
"Unit 309	Illinois"
"Mud Dobber	Texas"
"Happy Hermit	Canada"

"Skeeter Beater   Missouri"
"Double M La."
"AC 36   Illinois."
"Doug 1   Fla."
June 26, 1975
"V1E3, Bill New Brunswick, Canada"

"10-4 Canada, bring it on back to this Country Cousin, downtown, flatlands of Eastern North Carolina. You're walking tall."

"10-4 Cousin, you're blowing smoke. What are you running?"

Smiling, I could hardly wait to give them the goods news!

"Tram, Titan 2, MoonRaker 6 at 75 feet looking right at you."

"10-4 Cousin. You're 10-10 and wall to wall. Looks like about 20 over S-9."

"Roger thems good words Bill, What are you running?"

"Hey Cousin, what happened, you're in the dirt?"

I didn't have time to answer, my shack was filling with smoke. Frantically slapping at switches, turning buttons, (Del said later all she could hear was,

"My Stuffs gone, My Stuffs gone!!!!!! Damn, Damnit all to hell!!! What the hell's going on?")

She had run in the carport door and seeing all the smoke was hollering something about calling the Fire Department..........

"Never mind. My Varmit died."

"Your what?"

"My damn booster."

"Oh, I thought the house was on fire. If you don't need me, I'm going back to the shop."

"No, go ahead. I'll clean it up."

What I needed now was a Big shot of Bourbon on the Rocks served in a 55 gallon drum and a 5 foot piece of PVC pipe for a straw.

"What the hell am I going to do now?"

My Super Station without the Varmit was like "Screen doors on a Submarine".....it wouldn't work. I cleaned up the mess my baby made when the big paper caps went. The smell would be there for a while.

"Ever smell a transformer that gave up the Ghost? You got it."

That evening when Freddy got home, I was waiting.

"Hey Guy, be out shortly."

When he opened the shop and took one look at me, he knew I was sick. A lost puppy ain't never looked that bad.

"My Varmit died"

"Let's take a look at her."

By the smell, he already knew.

"Looks like the two big caps, I've got those, and the transformer. Bob, I'll have to order it."

"How long?"

"Probably a week."

Jesus Christ! What could happen next?

"Bob, maybe it's time to upgrade."

"Upgrade?"

"Yeah Guy, take a look at this."

He set the Siltronix 1011C in front of me and I immediately started drooling.

"You been on sideband yet?"

"No, something in the Tram won't let it go."

"Know anything about it."

"No, not really."

He went on to explain the theory and basically how it worked. Explaining that the un-needed sideband (upper or lower) and the carrier were suppressed. That way all the output was concentrated in your signal. He didn't have to explain about the "Ears" on a "Tube Type Radio", the Tram had shown me that. Maybe now was the time. He could allow me a good "Trade-in on the Varmit and Tram and I could step up a notch. What kind of trade? Freddy did just a little bit of figuring: $200.00. Thinking, God that ain't nearly as bad as I thought. I had $300.00 stashed from the sale of that used Hobart 410 slicer last week.

"Let's do it! But wait, I don't have the Tram."

"No problem, bring it to me in the next couple of days."

He spent a few minutes explaining how she worked and issued me a "November Charlie number, NC 1319. I got one for Crackerjack too, 1320. Freddy was in charge of issuing them in the eastern part of the state. His was: NC 88. He also strongly suggested that I "Listen in to learn how the sidebander's talked." Cousin had a LOT to learn. Freddy's handle on the AM side was "Davy Crockett". I don't think he had time to use it or, NC 88 or, as I would learn later, the many other numbers issued to him.

"ME AND MY 1011 CHARLIE'

"Bre……….ak 1-4 for Crackerjack."

"Bring it on, Cousin."

It was about 7PM and I was almost back to the home 20…..uh, QTH now.

"Crackerjack, are you loose?"

"Finishing up supper, whatcha need?"

"Got time to come over for a minute?"

"Guess so."

"Okay, bring Bo, Del's out of the kitchen."

"10-4, Crackerjack gone."

I'd swallow something whole while I was setting up "Charlie". She was a bit smaller than the Tram. I even gained a little extra space on the countertop. I had long ago closed the opening to the storage cabinets and Utility room and extended the counter at a right angle to the other wall adding 8 feet of top. "Charlie" looked just like she belonged. Making the necessary hook-ups, I powered her up. After tuning her, she was ready. I wasn't. I no longer had channel separation with clicks. Just had to guess where the center of the channel was. That was much easier on Sideband than "Ancient Mary". On sideband you just "Zero Beat" the frequency. On AM, you just tuned til it sounded right.

"Cousin, what in the world have you got now? What's that smell? I went through the whole thing with him. He kinda laughed,

"Didga blow it up on purpose?"

"Crackerjack, surely you don't believe………"

He was eyeing that spitting image of the "Thorn in his side" from up the road. For the most part, my beams had kept me from totally inferring with Crackerjack's station. I also tried every way possible to keep my signal clean.

"Go ahead, give that big knob a twist. He turned it clockwise very slowly passing by all the lower channels. The needle rising and falling as he passed the centers of each. Up around 405, there was a very strong sideband signal. Tuning in on it we heard HFX-8274 in Meridian Kansas in QSO with a station in Florida we couldn't hear. He was talking the way we used to before CB. No slang, no good buddy, no 10-4s nothing from AM. Almost sounded technical. Might a well have been, he was describing a di-pole he'd just built and was trying on 11 meters. Crackerjack said he sounded like he knew what he was talking about. One thing for sure, if he was talking on that piece of wire then, somebody knew what they were doing! We listened for a few minutes, then eased if up further. Up near the end of rotation at 455 we found another QSO. It was HFA-2810 in New York. The band was changing. It would drop out soon. Dropping back down to the lower 23, we scanned the channels stopping here and there. It was getting late when they went home. I still hadn't had a QSO. That could wait til morning.

It was about 3AM. Everything was quite. According to the weatherman, it was going to be a nice day. Del would be fixing breakfast around 8 and we'd be off to Sunday School and Church around 10.

I eased onto my barstool and fired Charlie up. The band was almost dead. I listened to a couple of eighteen wheeler's out on hwy. 11. They were northbound headed toward Greenville. "Too Hot to Handle" was loud! "Hot Rod" was easy to copy, but he sure won't loud. He'd just had a "Two tube box" installed and knew he was loud. If you'd passed him on the road when he had the mike keyed, he'd have blown your FM station right outta the mobile. Hot Rod was saying, soon as they got back to the Port

City, he'd have on too. I eased on up the band above 23. Road Runner was on channel 23B. He had a good signal once I put the Moon 6 on him.

"Breaker Road Runner."

"I'm broke, come on in."

"10-4, Road Runner. Good morning, what's your twenty?"

"Fort Eustis, Va., what's yours?"

This was real short skip. Didn't usually get into Virginia. Too close.

"Albertson, North Carolina, bout 75 miles east of the Capital City and about 75 miles from the coast. You got the Country Cousin."

"10-4 Country Cousin. You're walking tall up here in "Blue Blood Country". You got a copy on the "Corn Base" in Missouri?"

"Negative, he's on the side of the beam. Tell em to holler. I'll try to get him on the Super Scanner."

"10-4, hey Corn Base, give Country Cousin a holler down in North Carolina."

Nothing, as always, the skip was selective.

"You copy him Cousin?"

"Don't hear a thing, Road Runner, sorry."

"Okay, let me sign with him, I wanta see what you're running. 10-4?"

"Roger, Road Runner, go ahead."

He signed with the Corn Base and came back.

"Country Cousin, what in the world you running. Don't sound like most CB's"

"Road Runner, it's one of those converted 10 meter rigs called a Siltronix, 1011C. mike's a standard UG8-D104 driving a MoonRaker 6 up about 80 feet on a Rohn Tower."

"10-4, no wonder it sounds so good. I've heard about the 1011C and seen one MoonRaker six. You got some station."

"It's been an interesting past 6 months"

"Got any wallpaper. Sure love to get something from you."

"10-4, sure do. Gotta get it changed though. I says I got a Tram Titan Two. Just got Charlie on the air yesterday."

We exchanged A-D's and I Signed. After getting my second cup of coffee and probably 4th. Cigarette, oh yeah, I ate them til 1984. Dem Doral's were wonderful when you could quit coughing. Had to have one of them lit before my feet hit the floor. Then it would take the next 10 minutes to stop coughing. That first cup of coffee would help calm it down. In 1982, the septic tank lines in the old section of the house stopped up. When I took the "Clean-out" plug loose, out poured thousands of the plastic filter tips from the Dorals. That ended throwing "spent butts" in the "John". Everything in the house and cars was coated with nicotine. The smell was impossible to get rid of. As long as you smoked, you couldn't smell it and the nicotine made sure you didn't care.

I flipped over to sideband on the "lower side" LSB. Up around 395, I ran across HFX 3502 from Grand Turk Island in the West Indies. Eben had a strong signal once I found him. Using the Super Scanner for a general location and then putting that Moon 6 boom down their throats worked real well. Eben was running ham gear he'd modified to drop down into the 11 meter band. We had a good QSO, exchanged A-D's and signed. Just below I found HFX 5364 in Louisiana. Alvin was running a Charlie too. His had been converted to go all the way up to 10 meters. Freddy had said he'd be able to do that soon. We had a joiner from Texas, HF 7979, Jim had an excellent signal. We were all able to hear each other and talked about how bad (or good) the skip was and the season was just starting. Damn, its almost 7:30. Promised Del I'd take Wendi out for her morning stroll and wash the car off before we left for Church.

"Gentlemen, I have to sign, thanks for the QSO. November Charlie 1319 is QRT."

See how I'm already using that "Sideband" lingo. If you're going to dance on their floor, it will have to be to their music. I'd copied the "Q" list from something Don had when I went to see him about the tower.

Del always put the main course for lunch in the oven before we left for church. When we got back it was on the table real fast. We finished lunch, I headed toward the shack and she and Wendi went to Rose Hill.

The band was pretty wild, HFX 3195 in Illinois, then HFB 3107 in Maine, followed by NF12 in Puerto Rica and a local, WF1 on the mobile in Sneeds Ferry, NC., then another local, NC 308 in Newport, NC. HF 354 from New Brunswick, Canada blew in, then HCF 390 from Fla.

It went on and on. 30-Whiskey-828, 30-Whiskey-618, 30-Whiskey-895 and HFB-2922, all from Illinois. Then there was 29-Whiskey-2003 from Iowa. More locals, Unit 303 and 12-W-347 from Deep Run, NC. Knot-Hole-Charlie 96 came in from Richlands, NC followed by 12-W-472 in Midway, NC and 12-Whiskey-466 in Cape Hatteras, NC. The list grew, VHF 2502 from Florida, 27-Whiskey-62 in Fla., 27-Whiskey-59 in Fla., 18-Whiskey-3466 in La., 28-Whiskey-1215 in Texas. Locals again, Dixie Uncle 37 in Turkey, NC; CR-194 in Jacksonville, NC; ENC(Eastern North Carolina) 1 in Pink Hill, NC. Long again, CA-211 in Ark., Ranger Six in Kansas. Local again, ENC-6 in Goldsboro, NC; NC-2012 in Laurinburg, NC; NC-462 in Raleigh. Wow, what a day! I had no problem getting to bed that night

"BOB'S CB IS BORN"

Monday was another world. Say goodbye to the toys for a couple of days. Off to Greenville to work. I'd sure had my work on the back burner lately. That had to come to an end. Stopping in the Kinston Branch, I picked up some samples and catalogs.

"Mike, we going to have breakfast?"

"Sure, go on down, I'll be there shortly."

The waitresses saw me walk in. Getting my coffee, they knew exactly where'd I'd be. Number 13 was mine. I'd bought and paid for that booth many, many times. King's Restaurant was the best breakfast place in town. Victor King walked over to tell me about his new RV. He was always getting some new toy. It was an RV this time, next it would be a boat. There would be a Cobra in it along with a "Kicker". Between his RV's and boats he had plenty of toys. Later when he retired, he'd spend a lot of time in Florida on the RV. You could bet that his "sidekick" Arthur Johnson, retired restaurateur would be there too. He operated the "Baron & Beef just down the road for years until the doctor made him quit.

Sugar Bear arrived and set down. We ordered the usual, "Tenderloin Biscuits". We'd take half the biscuit, wrap it around the piece of tenderloin and have the other half to spread a pat of butter and packet of grape jelly on. That was a "GREAT" breakfast.

"You still thinking about going into business with Joe?"

"Yeah",

We'd kicked it around and came up with a good way of handling it. Probably would start soon.

"Think you can make any money at it?"

"Don't see how you can help it. Much business as there is."

"Guess you're right. I sure got enough in it. Did you get me a "Knot-Hole-Charlie" number?"

"Yeah, I got a block of them the other night. Give me a holler on Lower 16 when I get back Wednesday. I'll give it to you."

We started up to pay our checks.

"Hey boys, come on back here. Take a look at this."

Victor led us into the kitchen to one of the 40 gallon gas kettles.

"This thing's about had it. Can't seem to keep it fixed." David says that it's paid it's dues. Military surplus, at least 25 years old."

"Victor, let's drive a new one under it."

"Get me some numbers."

"You need them now?"

"Yeah, now."

"Mike, I'll see you later. Gotta go back to the store. (Oh, didn't I mention, this is also a goooood account)! "

I paid my check and went back to the store. Calling Raleigh, I got Dan Baker, the General Manager on the horn. He said we had one in the basement that had come in wrong for a job. He sure would like to get rid of it.

"What kind of gas?"

"LP I think, don't matter, we can change the orifices."

"Give me a number."

He discounted it pretty good for 1975. Wouldn't been close today in 1999. They'd laugh you out of the building. I copied a spec. sheet of the Groen AH 40 and took it back to Victor. Wilber Jr. had come in, (He was the other partner at that time.) They looked over the quote, shook their head approvingly and wanted to know when it would be delivered? The truck usually ran to Raleigh on Friday's to restock.

"Can't get it any earlier?"

"I'll try."

"Send it."

God, I'd already made my commission for this week and hadn't left Kinston yet. I turned the order in to Bill Dean, my boss. He said he'd take care of it. I left with a big smile on my face.

Now, all this time I've been upgrading the base. My mobile hadn't been going "lacking" either. She now sported a Siltronix 90 "Slider" to help my Panther go anywhere it wanted to. I'd upgraded my box to a Palamar 150. This mobile was 10-8. I checked into the Ramada, my home away from home then, usual room, 100 and rode over to the Three Steers Restaurant for lunch. Woody and Janie Smith have been the owner/operator's since Janie's dad, Wilber Hardee put them into business. You've heard of Hardee's, Little Mint's, Space House's, Little Rocket, Biscuitown USA, same man, he started them all. If there's ever been an "idea man", its Wilber Hardee. His worst problem, besides loving to spend money, is that as soon as he gives birth to a idea and get its running. He's bored. He's still around, "Born Again Christian" with a storehouse of memories. But that's about all. I still love to sit and talk to him. There's still that gleam in his eyes.

"Bob, this next project is going to be the one." (Nothing would make me happier, Wilber.)

Donna Ware, Director of Pitt County Schools Child Nutrition, called School Food Service then, joined me. She's been the director since 72 and really knows her stuff. We talked about some of the different school's needs. I made notes and referred to them later. Her office was located on the 4th. Floor of the Court House annex. I'd call on her the same time I called on the County Jail located in the same complex. I made a few more calls and decided to chop it for the day.

I caught Triple Nickel crossing town and signed as I pulled up in front of the room.

"Good talking to ya, Triple Nickel, catch you later, Cousin gone."

"40-Roger-4, Cousin, Triple Nickel listening in."

"Lord God", L.G. Deyton(Sugar Foot) had already checked in and was one up on me.

"Hey Cous, you ready for one?"

L.G. always stayed in the room beside me when he was working Greenville.

"Pour me one, be right in."

I threw my briefcase and coat into the room and walked into his.

"How goes it sir?"

"Bout the same. The damn "PYA" crowd keeps eating into my business."

L.G. was the "Food Peddler" for John Sexton Co. When I got into the business in 62, Sexton was "King of the Hill" with Seaboard Coffee Company out of Rocky Mount just behind them in Eastern Carolina. Robbie Collie, the then "Seaboard Coffee Rep." would own the Northeastern corner for years to come. Still does, although he's with another company.

"I know how you feel. Everytime I look around, there's another "Pot & Pan Peddler" knocking on my doors. Looks like they'd learn, this is my territory."

"Yeah, right. When we stopped using Company Trucks and started delivering on "common Carriers", its all been down hill. Ready for another?"

"Sure, have a good weekend?"

"Yeah, Mary Katherine ("MK") and I went to the Angus Barn Saturday night. We were about wasted when we finally got a table. Here."

He handed me my drink and set back down on the bed.

"How was your meal?"

"Who knows?"

We laughed. We'd both been there and done that before. A group of us back home had gone over to the Beef Barn in Kinston to celebrate something; birthday, anniversary, something. L.C. and Bo (Crackerjack & Little Bo Peep), Sandi & Max (Chipmonk & Miss Kitty), Lester Wood and Charlotte (Yankee Henry, Charlotte didn't want a handle), Del & I (Lady & Cousin) had split a bottle of Cold Duck before leaving home, or was it two bottles? I think Lester had had something else before they arrived from Raleigh. They pulled a couple of tables together and wanted to know if we'd like a drink before our meals.

"Absolutely!! Bring Cold Duck!"

Pearl, she usually waited on us. Brought over a bottle and glasses. One round almost wiped out the bottle.

"Hey Pearl, bring another."

Then it was another and another. By the time we got around to ordering, Lester and Del were "Real Happy". They were both up walking around the tables finishing off the nearly empty bottles and then our unfinished glasses. We got them back to their chairs long enough to order, then Del had to go to the Ladies room. She still wasn't back after we'd fixed our salads.

"Bo, please go check on Del."

When Bo opened the door, she broke out laughing. Del and gone in and maybe used the facilities, then started pulling all the paper off the rolls and stringing it around the room. She was sitting in the corner on the floor when Bo walked in. When she brought her back to the table, Del was extremely happy. So was Lester. I threaten to lock them both in the trunk of the car on the way back.

"No more Cold Duck, eat!"

After some food, they began to calm down. It was really a good evening.

OK, OK, one on me.

Each year, Del and I hosted our family reunion at home. It had begun as a "Pig Pickin" in the back yard with a canopy over a couple of tables for the food. The seating was limited, so you sat wherever you could. After the big Thunder Storm the second year, I promised myself, I'd be able to seat these folks inside one day. Years later, I fulfilled that promise. The crowd grew each time until the last year it was held, there were 125 invited guests. My brother Larry came up from Florida each year bringing family and friends. They'd arrive late Friday night and the party would start Saturday. His two step daughters loved to play cards and usually won. They'd stay up most of Saturday night with the crew cooking the pig. If there was anything to drink, and there usually was plenty, they'd slip around and get into it. A couple of times, they'd end up on the cots, sleeping it off. Tina and Sally were a lot of fun to be around. Just don't play cards for money. They'd take all of it. In 1981 when the new chicken house was completed, Ray threw a big party celebrating it's completion. Larry, Sheila and the girls happened to be visiting. We all walked over and joined in the festivities. There was a "Pig Pickin" along with all the trimmings and plenty of beer. Sally would stand beside me waiting for me to finish so she could get me another one. What we didn't know was that everytime she go, she'd gulp one down on the way back. She and I really got wasted. In fact, I got lost walking back to the house. Oh, Sally was fourteen at the time.

After spending two months cleaning and preparing, I was usually ready to party too. The "Pig Pickin" was always on Easter Sunday. That meant that the pig would go on the coals around mid-night Saturday. Before Larry Graduated from high school, he spent his junior and senior year working as a waiter at Joe West's Country Squire Restaurant. Getting one of those positions was something akin to being appointed "Page Boy" for the State Legislature. The experience polished him and also introduced him to many interesting and important people. The tips were always extremely good. Over the years when he came home. A night was always set aside for a trip back to the "Squire". This year would be no different. Lester and Charlotte had arrived earlier in the day and we had already gotten into something, beer maybe. Having my nephew Jeff around allowed me to be a little more at ease. There were so many things that had to be done in preparation. He was familiar with all of them. As the afternoon wore on. Lester and I (more me) had more drinks.............I awoke sitting in recliner in the den, it was dark and dead quite.

"What the Hell?"

My head was splitting. Getting up, I walked through the house, nobody. Out in the yard, nothing. It was a little after nine. It became very apparent, I'd gotten drunk and passed out in the recliner. They'd all gone to the Squire for Dinner. Four aspirin and two BC's later I survived, a little bit embarrassed, but, what the hell? It wasn't the first time.

L.G. and I mixed another.

"Howdy, kin a man come in for a drink?"

it was "4-J's", Joel Julius Johnson Jr. L.G. invited him in.

"Come on in, pull up a chair or bed and have one."

Joel poured one and grabbed the other bed.

"Been one hellova day. Ain't nothing gone right since I left Fayetteville. Damn fool pulled out in front of me south of Clinton and I damn near lost the mower's."

Joel traveled most of North Carolina for a golf course maintenance company. He almost always had a trailer behind his mobile with equipment on it.

"Then Damn fool Patrolman stopped me and gave me a ticket cause there won't no damn reflectors on the trailer. I'd loved to told him what I thought of his reflectors. He could have wrapped them in Barb Wire and shoved them up his Butt. Got over to the Country Club. Damn Pro was gone. I told him I'd be there at three. Left the trailer sitting right there. See if he can see it when he gets back."

"Time for another round, Cous, you going to eat supper tonight, or you gonna drink it?"

"Too early to tell, L.G., let's drink on it."

"What are you going to do Joel?"

"Nothing, let's go over to the bar and have a few."

We walked out of the room.

"Cous, what's all that crap in your car?"

"Crap, what crap?"

"That damn thing on the hump."

"That's my CB."

"Don't look like no CB I ever seen."

"Sit down in it, I'll show you."

Joel got in on the passenger's side. I fired her up and ran the slider up and down the channels.

"What the hell is that?"

"Sideband."

I tuned in on a strong signal up around 385. The station was in Kansas.

"That sure don't sound like mine, all I got is noise."

"Yeah, this is Sideband."

"What the hell good is it, can't talk to nobody."

"Sure you can, Unit 413, this is November Charlie 1319."

"Go ahead 1319."

"I've been out of the mobile this afternoon, how's the band been?"

"Opened up here around noon our time. Mostly east coast. Your signal's peaking S-5."

"You're S-9 on peaks. Thanks for letting me in, November Charlie 1319 clear."

"Unit 413 clear with NC 1319, 29-W-2444, go"

"What's all those numbers? How'd you do that on a mobile? I gotta get me one of these."

"That'll take two or three drinks to explain."

"I'll drink to that, lets go."

I don't remember whether we ate or drank our dinner. Probably both.

Tuesday was uneventful. We met back at the motel around 5 and repeated the night before.

Wednesday morning I had an appointment with Barbara Lewis, she was the School Food Service Director for Edgecombe County Schools (she retired last year). Barbara and I rode out to North Edgecombe High School and checked the Beverage Air milk boxes. School was closed for the summer and it was a perfect time to replace old equipment. Both SM 49's were in bad shape. They were at least 15 years old. She asked about repairing them.

"Barbara, it would be wasting your money. When you get one thing fixed, another will break."

She agreed.

"Okay, send me two."

We left North Edgecombe and rode over to Bullock. The serving line had been pieced together and didn't have a "Sneezeguard" or trayrail.

"What do I need to do here?"

I measured the units and told her we could fabricate the needed pieces.

"Good, take care of that for me too."

"Where to next?"

"Back to the office I guess. That will take care of me this time. You need to call me next week about Carver."

It was close to lunch. I suggested we stop at the Tarboro Inn.

"Sounds good."

As we were being seating,

"Bob Holt, where have you been? I've been looking for you for a month."

"Peg, all you had to do was call."

Peggy Wall was the General Manager. She came to the Tarboro Inn while it was still under construction. Russ Harris and Sam Clark, Jr. had just made one of the best decisions of their lives when she was hired. She was Inn Keeper at the Holiday Inn in Williamston when Russ hired her. She'd been on several other properties before and really knew her stuff. Living in Rocky Mount when she and her ex. Charlie, went their separate ways she was awarded the house but spent most of her time on the property she was managing at the time.

"The dishwasher's not doing right."

"Barbara, I'll be right back."

We walked into the kitchen to the dishwashing layout. Cycling it, I didn't see a problem.

"The rinse temperature won't stay up after two or three racks."

"Let's call Hobart."

"Is that all I need to do?"

"That's right, 1-800-682-2032."

"Thank you sir. Go eat your lunch, I'll take care of it."

I'd sold the job in 1971. Up until then, it was my biggest.

"Okay, Barbara, let's eat."

I'd had a great week. Time to go home.

"Yeah, yeah, what can I tell you. It's only Wednesday and I'm going home."

I stopped by Insurance Man's on the way home. Joe was sitting back in the recliner almost asleep.

"Knock, Knock, Joe. Can I come in?"

"Come on in cousin. How'er you doing?"

"Having a great week. Still interested in setting up something in Albertson?"

"Sure, sit down and let's talk about it."

We worked out the details and made a list of items for me to take with me. It included several radios, antennas, mikes and accessories. Anything else I needed, I'd just have to call and come get it. After loading my car, I headed for home.

"Where am I going to set all this stuff?"

The shack was already cramped as it was. Moving the draftng table to the other end offered space beside the steps. Del came in about six and asked about supper.

"What's all this stuff?"

"I'm in the business now."

"What?"

"Yeah, start making back some of the money I've spent."

I'm sure that sounded good to her.

Word spread quickly that I was in the business. I had customers instantly. They'd bring their trucks and cars by and leave them. I'd install their new toys and collect the Green Stamps.

Business was good. Joe and Del were happy.

"Joe, (on the land line) These guys want "heaters"."

"Bob, they'll get you in trouble. You have to be very careful who you sell them to. It will backfire on you. I'd rather not do it."

I understood how he felt, but the "box" was as much in demand as the rigs. I contacted "Benny's" and got them to send me a wholesale catalog. It listed all the "Boxes I was familiar with and a lot I'd never heard of.

Putting together a list, I placed my first order with them, COD. Now I had to find $1,400.00 before UPS arrived. Three days later,

"By God, I've got "Heaters" now.

I'd ordered several Palamars; TX-50's and 75's along with one Kriss-300M. They went like "Hotcakes". By the weekend, they were gone along with most of the radio's, antenna's and mike's. Monday morning I stopped by Joe's and settled up.

"Bob, you're doing great. Ready for some more?"

"Sure, more this time."

"Take most of what's here and I'll get some more ordered today."

I'd already re-ordered more amplifiers, doubling my first order. I was on open account now.

"Okay, let me know when it comes in. See you later."

I drove up to Raleigh to get the fabrication ordered for Barbara Lewis. I walked into Stainless Steel Fabricators (the fabrication arm of Montgomery Green Co.) and found Lester Greene, the Manager. His last name was Greene (spelled with an E) and wasn't related to the Green's of Montgomery Green who were Jewish. He never tried to imply that he was. Gene Green tried that when he came with the company as a salesman. Story goes that he and Mr. I.J., the founder and president were in the shop one day and he told Gene to walk with him over to one of the "Break-Presses" It was the "Old Man's" pride and joy, a two hundred fifty thousand pounder. Biggest one around.

"Okay Junior, haul it out."

"What in the world are you talking about, Mr. Green."

"Understand you want to be a relative of mine. I'm going to have to circumcise you first."

"Gene became a full-fledged Gentile again."

We walked into Lester's office.

"How's it going Bob?"

"Great, how bout you?"

"Same here, nobody's selling anything, if they are, they're giving it away, but what's different? How's Cbing?

"Doing good. I need to ask your opinion about something."

"Sure, go ahead."

"I've got this 75 foot tower,(I showed him a couple of pictures) and I need some way to lay it down to work on the antenna."

"That's quite a package. Bend your pocketbook?"

"Bend it, Hell, broke it!"

We laughed.

"Know how much it weighs?"

I pulled out the information and gave it to him.

"Going to have to think about it. Give me a couple of days. Got anything else?"

I showed him my sketches of the sneezeguard and trayrail for Barbara. He gave me a price and I ordered it.

"Where you getting your CB stuff?"

"Hell, I sell it Lester."

"What, why don't you tell somebody? I need one."

"Come on out to my office."

We walked out to the "Bird" and popped the trunk.

"Well, I'll be damn. You're weren't kidding, where you? I need something cheap to go on my mobile. What do you suggest."

"The Royce 1-600 was still the best buy along with a 173 Shakespeare."

"How much?"

For him, I cut it down to nothing. He'd done so many things for me since I came with the company.

"Hey, that's a good price. Want cash or check?"

"Cash always works better."

He paid me and I walked up to the store. Maynard Pearce was in the basement. That was the quietest place to take a break. He worked the sales desk out front with Billy Britt. Along with the telephone, they had their hands full. We talked a minute and I headed up the stairs. Billy was standing in the back talking to Jerry Barfield about some Syracuse China. Billy asked how things were going down east and Jerry wanted to know how the fishing was. I told him I'd check with some of the guys and let him know. My only fishing experiences were with the group from Williamston. We'd go down to Swan Quarter in the fall, put in at Oyster Creek, and fish out in the "Lower Middle Grounds" near some of the "wrecks" (ships sunk by the Military for bombing practice. If the red flags were flying, you kept your "ASS" outta there.) in the Pamilco sound. Other than that there had been that one experience when I went with Chuck Sledge, Carl Baldridge and a group from an Insurance Agency in Windsor on an overnighter. God, that was a fiasco. Spending the night in Mann's Harbor, we were going over to Wancheese and take their boat out the next day. That night we went over to the foot of the bridge and had supper at one of the seafood houses. That is, all but the Chinaman. Carl was in rare form. Full of jokes and other garbage and plenty of Jack Daniel's. He never did eat and when we got back to the rooms , he wouldn't go to sleep. I was left with him to baby sit. I dropped off after 3 and was awakened at 4.

"Time to get up! The fish are waiting."

We couldn't wake Carl up. He was as drunk then as the night before.

"Well, load him up. We can't leave him here."

We drug him out to the car.

"God, he smells terrible."

We had breakfast, all but Carl and drove over to the boat. It was a big one with plenty of room. We stored Carl on top of one of the fish boxes and went out through Oregon Inlet. Passing under "Bonner Bridge" was some experience. I'd been over it many times, but never under it. Arching from shore to shore, it was almost five miles long. It connected Nags Head and the mainland with Hatteras Island.

We trolled for Blues and Spanish. They'd be there, then they'd be gone. All in all, a pretty good day though. Around 2 that afternoon, Carl started stirring. He looked and smelled like he'd just come out of a "Crab Chum Pot". They sent him below to clean-up. He ate any and everything in sight. When he came back on deck, he was wide open. If he'd been any fuller of crap, he'd exploded. We listened to him all the way back to Windsor. I'd never been so happy to see my car in my life. I dropped my fish off for "Slow" to clean at the Town and Country. I'd split them with him half and half. I walked across the parking lot to my room, took a long shower, went back over to the restaurant, had a quick supper and went to bed. I was dead.

In Lacy Walter's office, we talked a few minutes. Pat Grady walked in……..

"Yeah, Yeah, give me a second."

Pat was someone you dreamed of waking up with. I'd known her in high school. She dated, and later married, Perry Lynwood Grady, I dated his sister, Gail. As the years went by, Pat blossomed. She was a sexy package now. The strawberry blond hair and a few freckles brought the Curves all together. Lacy would have given her the "Company" if she'd come across. That never happened. We talked a few minutes more and I walked into the Drafting Room. Kosky was involved with some big project and Mr. I.J. was in the corner with his "Brown Paper Bag". That's what he'd do a layout on. It was up to Kosky and the rest of the boys to transform it into a "Scale Drawing." I didn't see Yankee Henry, so I spoke and left.

Driving back home I had the chance to make a few contacts with the locals on sideband. Unloading all those goodies and with the UPS shipment made me realize that something had to happen. There just wasn't any room.

Sales were good, both with MG of K, (Montgomery Green of Kinston) and my CB sales. That Saturday, I walked out to the old tobacco barn sitting about a 150 feet behind the house. It hadn't been used for years, other than the shelters. They were crowded with relic's from the past. A plow here, a piece of cultivator there, chain, "Lupin horses" and tobacco trucks. Tobacco sticks were everywhere along with broken bottles, cement blocks and rotten tobacco cloth. Looked "Snakey" to me. Daddy came over and asked me what I was doing.

"Think I'm going to turn this into my CB shop."

"Good, its in good shape, just needs a little attention."

"Little attention hell, more like a major renovation."

He laughed and walked back to the house. I couldn't remember the last time I'd been inside the barn. The burners had been removed years ago. With no windows, its was dark in there. I pulled a couple of 100 foot drop cords from the house. Inside, cob webs and shedded snake skins. Mostly chicken snakes though, wouldn't hurt you. Just scare hell outta you! Brought back memories of "Barning Tobacco" At lunch and at the end of the day we'd hang the finished sticks in the barn. Some were still the old log types and all were very dark inside. I always hung the top, Okay, I'm lazy. There'd always be at least one girl passing the sticks on the inside. Dropping a piece of "dobbing" or something on the burners below and hollering "Snake" created havoc. Everybody flew out of the barn. I remember a couple of times, there really was a snake. I laid my hand on one and jumped off the tier poles bringing the person under me along with the snake to the ground.

The tier poles were low enough you had to bend over to get around. I brought a chain saw in that I'd used on tree limbs. Down came the first row of tier poles. These were the newer "built-up" kind rather than the older log poles. The wood was useless. Over years of use they'd turned brittle being heated so many times. I got the next two rows down and hauled them down into the woods at the end of the house. I spent the rest of the day moving and throwing away the "stuff" under the shelters. Daddy said there wasn't anything there worth saving. Sunday afternoon, I tore the shelter down. Most of it was leaning and too dangerous to try to repair. Sure looked different now. Didn't look "Snakey" with the junk gone. I'd had to stop several times to help someone looking for a CB or something. Couldn't let this get into the way of that. God, I was tired. Hadn't lifted anything heavier that a beer or microphone in so long.

Monday I went to Shepherd Electric Supply north of Kinston and bought a 60 amp. Electric panel, service head, cable, meter base and conduit. That afternoon I hooked up the service and called REA. They informed me that it had to be inspected before they could hook it up. I didn't know anything about an inspection. Crackerjack said I had to call Kenansville, he still had that information from the chicken houses. The inspector came out, confirmed I was the owner and that I'd done the work myself. Surprise, it passed. REA came out the next day and hooked it up. I wired up a couple of boxes for the drop cords. I was ready now. Running 100 watt bulbs to each corner really changed the look. Now I could tell what it really looked like. It had been built with rough sawn lumber when it was green and had dried to different thicknesses. I didn't know what I was getting into. First thing, pour the floor. Crackerjack and Chipmonk had poured the floor in the egg room, they'd show me how. After putting down the plastic and wire mesh, I called Barrus. What size and how thick? Crackerjack said at least, 4".

"16 feet x 20 feet and 4 inched thick."

"3000 lb.?"

"Crackerjack, what the hell is 3000 lb.?"

"Tell em, that's fine. Thats the ratio of mix."

"Yes, 3000 lbs."

"All right, have a check waiting for the driver."

"It'll be here."

That won't bad at all. Kinda messy, ruined a pair of shoes, but, what the hell? Next day I was on it.

"I'll be in here in no time."

Little did I know. What I knew about carpentry was in front of me, nothing behind. I'd built a cedar chest from a kit in Agriculture Class. It was for a project and I given it to Mamma. L.C. told me I needed to put up firring strips to hang the paneling on. After he explained it, it made sense. I'd already done the wiring, so after the insulation, the paneling was next.

"Whoa Bob, you need to put the ceiling up first. Ceiling? Oh yeah, the second floor. I ordered 2 x 8's from Grady's. I know, shoulda been 2 x 10's, they cost too much. They were delivered the next day. When I got home, didn't take long to realize how heavy those 16 footers were. Working alone made it very interesting. I'd pull them into place with rope thrown over the remaining tier poles. Finally they were all in place with the opening for the stairs. I'd laid it out with a wall separating the steps and little storage room from the main room. Next came the ceiling strips to attach the 12" x 12" tiles to. After that I studded up the wall for the storage room and steps. It was coming together. The insulation was easy, then the paneling. Cheap Luan Mahogany. Well, it covered the walls. The overhead installation of the ceiling tiles was extremely tiring . finally it was done.

"Looking good!"

I brought Del out and showed her my handiwork. I didn't mention all those tools I'd purchased to build this with.

"Heck, it was just the cost of doing business. She didn't have to know everything."

Her remarks were positive. I felt good about that. Where had the week gone? I hadn't done enough in my territory to say I'd been there. Next week would be different.

Now don't misunderstand. I know I haven't said much about talking skip the past week. I'm having to do that early in the mornings. The solar indices were high every day now. Solar Indices? Later. There was skip bout anytime you wanted to talk it. The early morning kept you mostly on the east coast, up into Canada and the maritime provinces and down to Florida and the Caribbean. There were plenty of folks to talk to. I was always running into folks that knew a bunch more about radio that I did. HFB 1647 stationed at "Gitmo" Bay, Cuba was working on his "Ham" license. I'd have to look into that.

Monday I looked through my mail and found a letter from Lester, no faxes back then,. Inside was a detailed drawing of a pivot bracket and specifications for the pivot stand. Man, it really looked professional. Length of pipe, diameter, material and how it worked. The stand would have the pivot attached to the tower at 20 feet. There would be a fifty five gallon drum attached to the bottom with 42 gallons of water in it. It would be balanced and take very little to lay it down. The Stainless steel pivot bracket would be ready next time I was in Raleigh. I made several copies. Time to go to work. Foss and I had breakfast at King's and headed out. I stayed in Ahoskie at the Tomahawk Motel that night. Never was much to do there. As usual, I had a good meal across the street at the Tomahawk Restaurant. Odie Bracey came over and joined me while I waited for my meal. There were several items he wanted to go over with me next morning. After going to Roanoke Chowan Hospital next morning, I came back to see Odie. He really needed to replace his Char Broiler.

"Bob, there's gotta be a way to fix it."

I called Maynard and asked for pricing. It was an Ember Glo 41F.

"Okay Bob, here you go but he's not going to like it."

There were several hundred 7" round ceramic rods and stands in there for the coals to sit on.

"Odie, the replacement will run you $400.00."

"Uh, that hurts."

"How old is it?"

"Ten years old."

"Odie, its time to bury her."

He knew that, but didn't want to spend that kind of money.

"How much?"

"$2,500.00."

"Golly, Bob, that's high."

"Odie, look at what you're getting."

"I know, but golly………Okay, send it to me. How long will it take?"

I called Raleigh again.

"Its in stock, they'll deliver it on Wednesday."

"Okay, might as well tell them to bring 4 cases of water and 4 cases of iced tea too."

"Maynard, send it, along with 4 cases of 1410's and 4 cases of 1406's. Remember to put eight on it." (8 was my sales number.)

I stopped in Windsor to see Joanne before going on to Greenville. She was out in the schools. Leaving a card with a note on it, I went on to Williamston. Dan Bowen, Child Nutrition Director for Martin County Schools told me to come on in. There were good times to call on Dan and bad ones. You could never tell which one until it was too late. He needed a dishwasher and didn't want to use State Purchase and Contract. After visiting the school, I wrote up a quotation for the machine. I told him, Lester would have to come by and look at the dishtables. He was due in town on Thursday. I got to the motel at six. The party had already started. "Lord God, 4J's and Candy Man were getting it on. I poured doubles and caught up pretty quick. Lester showed up about 8. Boy, was he behind. (Lester was never behind, his milkshake cup never had milkshake in it. One time he walked into the bar at the Ramada, spoke, sat down and treed the gal at the next table, that's like when a dog runs a squirrel up a tree and barks til somebody comes up and shoots him. Nothing like the time we were "Coon Hunting" back behind the mill pond. Won't long before the dogs started baying. We crawled through the bushes and brambles, now remember It's night. You don't hunt coons during the day. Looked like the top of the tree was dead a probably hollow. Lewis Lee crawled up to punch him out so the dogs could get to him. He'd found the coon asleep and somewhere down in his infinite wisdom decided to stab him with his hunting knife. Now folks, that was the wildest thing you ever saw. When the blade hit that coon, he came outer there with the "pedal to the metal", bringing Lewis with him to the ground. The dogs went wild. They were sure it was the biggest coon they'd ever treed and they all wanted some of him. In the melee that followed with all the screaming and hollering, the coon got away. Anyway, Lester had treed her. Nice looking gal, all the stuff where it belonged, nice. She was drinking the durndest concoction I'd ever seen. Scotch and milk. Now remember, we're in North Carolina, ain't no liquor by the drink til some years later. We've got what's called brown bagging. You brought the booze with you and paid just as much for ice and a mixer as you would later for the real thing. He being the observant soul that he was, realized she was about to run out of scotch. Helpful was another of his many attributes.

"Bobby, I'll be right back"

I figured he'd gone to the head to take a leak. Walking back in, he was carrying, you guessed it, a full pint of Scotch. Problem was while he was gone, the gal's 250 pound Gorilla friend had arrived with his own Scotch. I walked over to the bar and asked Patrice to bring Lester a glass of milk. He'd hear about that bunches of times. I told him about Martin County, closed the business books and partied. We closed the bar at 2, walked, did I say walked, we crawled across the street to the Waffle House and had an early steak breakfast. As usual, up at six, 4 aspirin, 2 BC's, shower, shave, go to work. Oh yes, I could do it then. NO MORE! I drove over to Washington City Schools and called on Kay Finch, Child Nutrition Director for the City Schools. Kay was extremely loyal to me over the years. I could always expect to come away with an order. I stopped by Beafort Country Schools to see Sarah Cutler, Dietary Director of the County Schools, she was out in the schools working. Over at Beaufort County Hospital, Mr. Hicks placed a nice smallwares order with me. We looked at the dishwashing layout and discussed making some changes. Bill Misner, one of our engineers would have to look at that. I made one more stop at Elks' Rest Home. Mrs. Elks was always a joy to call on. When she bought something, it was from me. I took the back roads to Kinston. Down 17 through Chocowinity, grabbed the shortcut by the VOA site to 102. Crossing 43 at Calico to Stokestown Crossroads, left, then right through Cox crossroads to Hwy. 118. Straight to Grifton, then left on eleven to Kinston. I stopped by Joe's on the way though, picked up my goodies, looked at his GMC pickup he wanted to sell and headed home. On the backroads again, passing Tull's mill, I was almost there. Well, maybe 5 miles.

After unloading the car, I walked over to the Beauty Shop to say hello to Del and Windi, I changed clothes and walked out to the barn. I made a list of the materials to build the counters. J.W. Grady assured me that it would be there tomorrow. You took anything J.W. said with a grain of salt. (He will come up again.) Friday it did finally get there. I was really too busy Wednesday and Thursday with CB customers to do anything anyway. The service bench was cantilevered leaving all the space under it for open storage. Service Bench? Yeah, I was beginning to "service the rigs" a little bit. Mostly it was for wiring the Mikes. The display counter in the middle of the floor was enclosed with a gate for me to enter the service area. After a couple of weeks the open space had to go. Some folks just ain't honest. I used a small 2" grid wire to section it off. The sign above the service bench read. $20.00 an hour, $50.00 with your help. I'd seen that type of sign before. Now I knew why. Most of the time, Crackerjack, Chipmonk, Monkey Wrench or one of the group was always on hand to show everybody around. They all wanted to see the MoonRaker and the Shack. I didn't mind anybody going in long as "One of the boys" were around. I'd stuck up the old Ground Plane behind the shop. Mostly I used the "Dummy Load". (a one gallon can with transformer oil in it.) you could shoot it with a hundred watts with no trouble. That was the best way to check the power output and the modulation. You didn't bother anybody.

That Saturday morning I'd driven over to Don's in Beulaville to check on a rig I'd sent over to be repaired. We were talking about the MoonRaker and how pleased I was with it's performance. Skip was so bad you couldn't talk locally, especially on the mobiles.

"Bob, it you really want to get out locally, you need one of these. We walked out to his truck. There was a mobile in there about the size of a 1-600 Royce. He picked up the microphone.

"Break 76 for a radio check, WA4-UMH."

"Go Don, WA4-TUQ."

"Herman, I've got someone here I'm showing 2 meters to. Tell him where you're at."

He was just outside Goldsboro on his mobile. We then heard from Raleigh, Garner, Rocky Mount, Greenville, Kinston and Pink Hill.

"WA4-MHA, Pink Hill."

"Hey Pete."

Pete who? Pete Williamston.

"Hell, I know him, he's my cousin."

"Pete, got your cousin here. Bob Holt."

"Hey Bobby (I'll be Bobby to some people for the rest of my life.) Some radio, huh."

I agreed, Don signed and we walked back inside. I still didn't believe what I'd just heard. No noise, no nothing. Just clear voices no matter where they were. Don explained.

"It's called 2 meter radio and its FM. Just like the broadcast radio in you home or car. When the frequencies are that high, they're called "line of sight". If your antenna can see another antenna, you can talk. It's not effected very often by skip. What you just heard was the "76" repeater machine located on the channel 7 TV tower in Grifton. Each time someone transmits, the signal goes to the tower and is repeated or re-broadcast from 1,470 feet. The transmit and receive frequencies are offset 600 kHz. I had no clue what he was talking about. Thats how you can work all of eastern Carolina with 5 watts. The repeater is owned by the "76" ham group. The club's given the space on the tower to use because hams are very important during emergencies, natural or man-made, like hurricanes, when all other communications are down. We're there to help. God, I'd never heard of any of this.

"You outta try it."

"Okay, how?"

" You've got to take a test. It involved sending and receiving Morse Code."

That was no big deal. I'd learned that in the Boy Scouts. He explained the different levels.

"Order the Technician."

I'd bypass the Novice. Later when the test came in. the Code was a breeze, but the "technical" blew me away. When the results came back I was devastated. FAILED. I registered for Herman Civils electronics class at the start of the fall semester at Lenoir Community College. More about that later.

Del's brother was a metal worker. After a busy day in CB sales Saturday and Church Sunday morning, we went to see Dean and Mary Lou. Trying to explain what I wanted without seeing the tower wasn't working. Dean said he'd be down Monday after work to look at it. July was gone and we were into August. Everytime the TV weather man was on, seemed all he could talk about was the Hurricane Season. Nothing out there yet but….Look Out, They were coming. Sunday night brought Night Hawk, Speed Queen and Wesley over. We had Fondue. Its a lot of fun if you've got enough forks. They sure enjoyed it. Later, we were invited to go with them to eat steamed oysters. I had brought some home a few weeks ago and steamed them in the back yard. They were good and we were ready for the Oyster Bars. No, Del wasn't, some weeks later, we joined Vondee and Lexine, Night Hawk & Speed Queen, at Waller's in Kinston. When the Shucker's dumped those beautiful "Grade A Select" oysters in front of Del, steamed just right, she tried. Even with the help of 10 crackers and half a Pepsi, No Way! They was too juicy and too big. Those little ones I steamed, VERY WELL DONE!, were not like these. We had a good laugh. They brought her some fried ones and she was fine. Me? Nat Van Norwick introduced me to them a few years earlier on the banks of Pamlico Sound at a Vender's get-to-gether. J.T. Manning of Garner, Wynn and Manning hosted it. Nat had insisted I would enjoy it. You know, after a few drinks, I fell right into it. Nat got real tired of shucking them for me. You outta seen me trying to eat steamed crabs the first time. Far as I could tell, the yellow was as good as the rest.......until somebody told me, you didn't eat that stuff!

Monday proved to be a busy one out in the territory. I got home around 5 and had a yard full of CBer's waiting. Dean arrived about the time I finished with them.

"Damn Bob, what in the world have you got?"

We walked around the house and looked at the tower.

Okay, I understand what you need. He took down some scribbled some notes on a piece of paper.

"I'll call you tomorrow.

Dean called Tuesday night with a estimate. He listed everything he needed including 20 bags of "Sakcrete". His estimate seemed very reasonable to me.

"When can you do it?"

"Bob, this Saturday's the earliest."

"Lets do it."

"Okay, see you then."

Now I had to go to Raleigh to get the bracket. Next morning,

"Lester, Bob, I'm going up your way tomorrow to get the bracket. Need anything?"

Don't hurt to ask.

"Yeah, I need a little something to help me get out. Know what I mean?"

"I'll have it with me."

Thursday morning when the shop opened, I was there.

"Get up kinda early don't ya Cousin?"

"I get up early every morning. Skip's best when everybody else is asleep."

"Guess so. What you got for me?"

We walked back over to the car. Popping the trunk, I pulled out a TX-50, the TX75's and 150's were staring back at him. Pays to advertise, don't it?

"Lester, this will get you going."

"How much?"

"$75.00."

I told him he was getting the same special price I'd let him have the CB for. Looking at the other units, he wanted to know how much?

"One hundred and one fifty."

He grabbed up the "150" along with the jumper cable I handed him, tossed it behind the seat in his truck and we went inside.

"Bob, this is happy money. Happy cause momma don't know about it."

"Know exactly what you mean."

On the floor beside his desk was the "Bracket". Now folks, that was a fine looking piece of Custom Fabrication.

"Lester, that's beautiful!"

"It will do a good job for you. Remember, The whole system was designed for what's there now. Its not designed for any additions."

"I understand, (Hell no I didn't, later I'd prove that.) How much I owe you?"

"You can't afford it. Let me know how it works."

He told me those exact words many times and each one of them was for something very special. He's one of those special friends you're very lucky to have.

Picking up the bracket, I thanked him again and left. Barbara Lewis was on my list to see about Carver School. Luckily she was in. We rode over to Carver. The kitchen was totally inadequate for the increased enrollment that had taken place over the years. We discussed some possible changes and equipment additions. Work space was a major priority. I took some measurements so I could study it later. After dropping her off, I stopped by the Tarboro Inn.

"Peg, did you get the dishwasher fixed?"

"Bob, they came that afternoon. I'm happy now."

"Happy? That mean you don't need anything?"

"Need Anything!! Bob Holt, you and Ryland Sweeney sold me enough Black Lace China, Old English Flatware and Wilton

Armatel to last me a hundred years. Hell no, get outta here. Oh, while you're at it, send me 3 cases of 3 ½ oz wines. I need them for a reception."

"Three cases of 3769's on the way. Thanks Peg."

I stopped off at Joe's, gave him some money and picked up some other stuff. I couldn't keep my eyes off his truck. I had a ford pickup, just didn't like it.

"Joe, what's the absolute bottom."

He had it right this time.

"Done, I'll get back over this way later in the week and pick it up." When I got home, I called the guy interested in mine and made the deal. He came by later that evening and between CB sales completed the deal. Miss Kitty had a Notary stamp and was close by. I had one but couldn't use it "for personal use". A couple of years earlier I'd co-signed a note with my sister's daughter, Pam for a car. It was a used "Beetle" and would serve her purposes just fine. A couple of months into the contract I came home one day to find the car parked in the back yard. I called Clystia that night to find out what was going on. She didn't know, Pam was gone. Gone my Butt, what the hell was I going to do with the car? Not her problem. I called Luther the next day. No, she hadn't made any payments, they're were getting ready to call me. In 1959, I'd gotten a tattoo when I was in the Air Force. I thought it was on my forearm. Hell no! it had to be on my forehead and it didn't say "GERI". It said "SUCKER". In 1999 it must still be there. I call it the Robert F. Holt syndrome. Like it or not, I got it and I guess I always will. Sandra helped me fill out an application to become a Notary. Wasn't long before the car was gone. I was so busy, I didn't know what day it was. Friday, was it Friday? I went to the store. Bill said he needed a CB.

"What kind do you want?"

"Don't matter, just put it in."

Sugar Bear pulled Bill's Pontiac inside the back and in an hour, "The Pipe Smoker" was 10-8 and 10-10. Bill paid me, thanked both of us and pulled out for Wilson. Musta had a tee time at Wilson Country Club.

"Mike, breakfast is on me. Let's go."

We had our usual along with a helping of Victor and Mr. Arthur with his ever present cigar. He smoked it til the doctor said.

"Do it and die!"

Last time I saw him, he still had it. Hadn't lit one in years though.

"Foss, what are you doing today?"

"Nothing really, probably go back to the store for awhile."

"How bout helping me?"

"No more pine trees!!!! Other than that, Whatcha need?"

"I bought Insurance Man's truck and need to get it home."

"Lets go. I wanta see the tower anyway."

We stopped by Joe's, ragged awhile and took off for home.

"Bob, that's a bunch of antenna."

"It sure is, works good too."

We walked inside for a demonstration, He'd put up a PDL Quad earlier and was amazed at the "ears" on the MoonRaker."

"That's a hellofa antenna."

I carried him out the shop, he hadn't seen it either.

"You bout to be in business."

I sure was. I'd be in it tomorrow doing business. Del would be happy about that. She hadn't had the house to herself in months.

"Foss, I hadn't told you about this one."

I showed him the pivot bracket and the drawings.

"All right! I knew you'd figure out how to get thing down on the ground."

The 6 PM news startled me. A hurricane was off the south coast. Projected to make landfall Sunday or Monday. God! Shades of Hurricane Hazel. I was thirteen then but I vividly remember her. It blew almost all the trees in the yard over. Looked like a "War Zone" when it was over. I went out when the eye passed overhead thinking it was over. With no electricity for the past few hours, we didn't know anything about the eye. Out in Pink Hill,

Mr. Lee took advantage of the quiet and went to the "outhouse", the first winds of the other side blew the outhouse away leaving Mr. Lee sitting there for all the world to see.

This made tomorrow that much more important. I called Dean to make sure he was coming.

"Be there around 7"

I was waiting when he pulled up.

"Morning Bob, heard about the storm?'

"Yeah, hadn't everybody? You going to get it done in one day?"

"Sure, no problem."

If he could figure out how to get rid of me, it would be a breeze. I was all over him. He put me on the end of a shovel and that took my attention for awhile. When the 5 holes were ready, he put a 25 foot section of pipe in each. He'd backed the big truck up to the tower and had a ladder sat up on the bed. Those big trucks with 4 wheel drive didn't have any problem in the sandy land. Using a level, clamps and me, he aligned the first two and "spot-welded" them. Lining up the other three, he "spot welded" them. Now he was ready for the cross-member. The bracket was already on it. Checking several times, he made the connection.

"Time for the concrete Bob"

He came down and checked all the alignments.

"Okay, Bob, do your thing."

I dumped "Sakcrete" and water into each hole. Four bags per hole. Dean kept checking. He sure knew what he was doing.

"Okay Bob. She's gotta set up."

He solid welded each joint.

"Won't take long with the "Sakcrete"."

"Tomorrow?"

"Not if we don't have to."

"Dean, the storm's coming."

"Yeah, I know. I'll be here before it does."

I gladly paid him, really wanted to hug his neck, but he's too damn big to hug, like a football player. After he left, I walked out to the shop. It was around 3 and the guys were already coming in. Of course, they all wanted to see the "Pivot". Musta been a hundred people see it the next two days.

"Storm still coming, be here Monday night. Take all precautions and make all preparations."

"All right!, I have and I'm ready."

I hadn't secured another thing but the tower was almost ready. Dean called about 8 and said he'd be over late Sunday afternoon and cut her loose. Be sure to put the water in the drum. Water in the drum? I'd forgotten about that. He'd welded a couple of brackets on the bottom section for the drum to rest on and we'd attached it with stranded cable. It took a little while to measure and run the 42 gallons. I put the plug in and she was ready.

I followed the storm all day Sunday. Not much activity around the shop after church. Guess everybody was getting ready for the storm. Dean arrived about 4. I had already attached the "Come-A-Long" It only took a minute to cut the 3 posts loose with the torch. Nothing happened.

"Dean, is it loose?"

He walked over and gently tugged on it. It moved. I freed the guy wire and Dean pulled on the base. Gently, it started over. There was no strain on the wire at all. Lester Greene had done his homework and calculations without a flaw. It was perfect! I slowly let it down on the "T" bar stand we'd built for it. There was hardly any weight on it. We tied it down and went inside.

"Dean, have a beer."

I'd bought a case for him to take home. I was a very happy and very relieved man.

The hurricane? It was a bust. Damn near nothing. It had stalled (Okay, she) and turned to the northeast.

That was the first of many times the tower laid down until I finally overloaded it and , yes, it broke. That was in the future.

Bob's CB was off and running. Business was excellent. I had all I could do and more. I'm not complaining though. It certainly was helping me recover from my past year's expenditures. September was here and I had enrolled for evening classes at LCC. Tuesdays and Thursdays were now locked up. Although I only audited the classes, from the beginning I learned a great deal. I was putting all that new found knowledge to work on my bench. No, I never did understand the theory. I did have enough grasp to be able to read the schematics and trace the circuits although with CB repair 90% of the time, it was either the power transistors in the finals or the modulation transistors. If it turned out to be something else, you had to work for it. If it was the "Finals", There was always a culprit causing it and most of the time it was a faulty antenna installation and faulty coax problems. Both were easy to trace and repair or replace. Like me in the beginning, we didn't know what we were doing, but it sure looked simple. Then "Bang", bring money.

"DUPLIN COUNTY CB CLUB"

One of the really nice things to come out of the "CB Craze" were different clubs that began to spring up all over the country. Anytime you traveled the Super Slabs on a holiday weekend you'd almost always run across "Rest Stops or Coffee Stops" hosted by the local CB clubs. It was an opportunity to help, or give back. Almost all the CBer's I knew were extremely patriotic and good Samaritans. Given the opportunity, they were there to be called on. This was the first opportunity they'd been in a given in a long time and they were taking full advantage of it.

Duplin County CBer's were no different. If I remember correctly, Super Bee was the first president and Squirrel was the Secretary. There were quite a few members covering the county and some members over my way outside of it. We voted at one of the first meetings to get matching vests to wear. The vests were burgundy and had our handles on front and club name patch on the back. A lot of members were also members of other clubs and organizations, some pertaining to CB. I had joined several QSL "swap" clubs. Miracle Swap QSL and Wiggly Worm were the first two I joined. Sending in some of your cards brought many, many different ones from other members. On joining you'd receive lots of other goodies including patches. I'd sewn quite a few on my vest. July, 1975 brought the first CB Jamboree in the east. It was held at Pender Park on Hwy. 24 between Cape Carteret and Morehead City. Pender Park was a very nice campground for RSV's and "Tent Campers". There was a small lake in front that afforded an opportunity to "Paddle Wheel" around it. The club created a lot of interest in the jamboree and quite a few of us made plans to go. Available rooms that time of year "the Peak Season" were hard to come by and most ended up in Morehead City rather than on the beaches. That was really OK because we were going to spend most of our time at Pender Park. We arrived Saturday morning, spending most of the day at the Jamboree. Since check-in wasn't until 3PM, we waited until then to go into Morehead. By that time we were ready for a short rest. Checking in, that's exactly what most of us did. Coming back to life around 5,

"Where are we going to eat? I'm hungry. Let's decide."

"Okay, what do you want to eat?"

There were about twelve or fourteen in our group and the answers were as varied and the count.

"Okay, Okay, Steak and, or Seafood, Right?"

"Right."

At least we agreed on that. Yankee Henry and I had already decided that Mrs. Russell Willis Restaurant was the best place. Max Warner, who traveled Carteret County for Montgomery Green had said many times that it couldn't be beat. The times I'd been with Max always proved him right. Mrs. Russell Willis's, it would be.

We all loaded up and drove over to the Restaurant. As usual, there was a line. Mrs. Willis's daughter Mona recognized me and took down our number. While standing in line, now some of us had had a little nip, or two, we must have seemed happy to every-body around us. I couldn't help noticing several ladies looking at the vests and the patches on them. One of them came up to me and timidly asked?

"Do you really swap?"

It took a moment or two for the real meaning to sink in. She was talking about partners, not cards. I broke out laughing.

"Absolutely, would you like to join our club?"

You know, I think she would have. You could almost see the letdown in her eyes when I explained what the clubs actually exchanged. That really added to the atmosphere and made the evening.

One of the other clubs close by, Lenoir County CB Club purchased a "Closed box" truck and used it to perform different functions for the community. They also furnished communications for the East Carolina Council Spring Camporee held at the "Bonner North Scout Reservation" just east of Washington, NC located on the Pamlico Sound. It was beside one of the first Weyhouser planned community projects in the area called, Pamilco Plantation. Special friends of mine, live there. Donald and Lula Joyner. Donald's been the PYA rep. in the area forever, okay since the seventies.

Hammer Head and Bulldozer were always there helping with communications and anything else they were needed for.

The Scout office, being aware of my tie to CB's and my somewhat limited art abilities (Thank You Mr. Luther.) asked if I could make a plaque for Bulldozer. I, of course accepted and then wondered what I could come up with. Bulldozer was a very special person to me. This was one of the first opportunities to do "Public Service" and he was totally dedicated. After giving it a lot of thought, the idea of incorporating a radio and microphone in the plaque would be perfect. Digging through the box of discarded rigs, when I told someone they needed to trash one, most of the time they'd hand it to me. I'd throw it into a box and carry it to the trash when it filled. I'm not completely sure, but I think the one I chose was a Royce, 1-602. That was for no other reason other than the front looked good. I sawed the front off just back of the face and mounted it on a wood plaque. I used plastic letters and heavily coated it all with EZY-POUR. The finish was almost mirror-like. I wasn't at the presentation, but I understand Bulldozer was deeply moved. He thanked me many times afterwards. Its one of those things you do and it makes you really feel good inside.

"RAINBOW FERTLIZER"

As the fall began, so began the school year. My busiest season was school opening. Most orders had been placed at the end of the school year to be delivered now. With the lunchrooms being closed all summer, that also brought many other problems. Refrigeration especially suffered. I usually started my rounds in Pamlico County and worked my way up and around. The needs were very light in Bayboro, so I headed north to "Little Washington". The skip hadn't slowed much, but some. I ran the front door from Grantsboro over to Hwy. 33 and on to Chocowinity for several eighteen wheelers hauling lime. The Bug Stomper stayed so close on my backdoor, I thought several times he'd just come in. He and Gogitter ran five or six loads a day from Arapahoe to Pitt County and beyond. They were paid by the load. Didn't no grass grow under their feet. In Washington, Kay was having problems with a Glenco 2 door refrigerator over at P.S. Jones and wanted me to take a look.

"Kay, the compressor running but it's not cycling."

"What does that mean?"

"I'm not a serviceman Kay, but it looks like the compressor's gone."

The model number told you it was at least 15 years old. The ALA 40's had been discontinued some time ago.

"How much?"

"Probably around $1,500.00 dollars."

"When can I get it?"

After telephoning, I told her 10 days.

"Send it."

We went over to Tayloe then. The dishwasher was acting up.

"It's not the dishwasher Kay, it's the booster."

"Booster, how do you know?"

"It kicks the breaker every time it comes on."

"What do I need to do?"

I told her we could get the serviceman over but it would be several days. Phoning confirmed that. She didn't know what she was going to do. I told her I'd check on her Wednesday when I came back through.

I drove down 264E. to Swan Quarter. Now friends, you got to want to go there. Its highly unlikely you'd just wander by. Its a good hour out of Washington, more like one and a half at regular speed. Most times, there ain't enough traffic to have a "front or back door." You're on your own cept fer the "Little Radar Box" looking out your front door. After passing Belhaven, you just straddle the white line and bring her on. Passing Wart Hog down about the old Worth Moore's motel, he said it was clean and green all the way to Engelhard. Now Swan Quarter's in the woods but Engelhard's in another country. Don't believe me. Drive down there, try talking to them good folks. They speak another kind of English. We call'em "Hoi-Toider's" I really love their brogue. Problem is they're so "klanish", they won't talk to "Outlanders". When I first started traveling the "Outer Banks", coats and ties were required attire, no exceptions. When those fine folks saw you in a coat and tie, they knew you were either the "Feds or Revenuers". If it hadn't been for Dick Greg, He and his wife Annie owned, operated, and lived behind the Reef Restaurant on the causeway between Manteo and Whalebone junction on Nags Head. He was just across the road from the Oasis Restaurant. "Home of the Barefooted Coeds" Dorothy Kellom was quite an operator. She'd been the reason for my first trip to the "Outer Banks" a few years before, purchasing a Hobart VCM-40 to cut up onions for her

"World Renown Lace Cornbread". It really was delicious. Dick just took a like'n to me and took me under his wing. I really was just a good drinking buddy. I wouldn't be there long before he'd load me up and we'd go to the local Shrine Club or the Drafty Tavern back by the bridge. He'd holler to Annie something bout we'd be back in a minute. She go to "Cussin" and she was good at it. Of course she knew it would be hours before we'd get back. Usually the 5:00 PM rush would be well under way before we'd return. He'd always invite me in for dinner and I'd respectfully decline and get the hell outta there. Won't no way I wanted to hear Annie's wrath. I'd go on up to the Sea Ranch Motel. Shirley would check me in and I'd be in the Bar in minutes. Alice Sykes owned and operated the property. She was in her sixties when I met her and already had three face lifts behind her. When she'd come in for her evening drink, she'd always be attractively dressed, makeup perfect. By the time she left, totally wasted, she'd be a mess. Now Annie could cuss and looked the part. Alice didn't look the part when she came in. She'd get there quickly though. She also had a command of that part of dirty words that a lady wouldn't touch. It only took a couple of times and you were used to both of them though.

I've got to share this one with you. Daddy used to tell this story. Back in the mid-thirties, he'd go to the "Outer Banks" with Plunkett, my grandfather and Uncle Rommie. They'd be on a Model T. The roads won't paved back then and there were no bridges, only ferries. As now, from the time you'd leave Belhaven all the way to the coast, there'd be canals on both sides of the road. On one trip, they were between Stumpy Point and Mann's Harbor and had stopped to "Take a Leak". While they were standing there, two bear cubs swam across the canal and came up to them. It seems a good idea to take one of them along for the rest of the trip. As soon as they grabbed it, the screaming started. From across the canal in the heavy undergrowth came a roar and thrashing that was unbelievable. Mamma Bear was on her way. They jumped into the car just as Mamma crossed the canal. She rushed up to the car. The first swipe took the radiator cap and ornament, the next one took one of the head lights. THEY GAVE THE CUB BACK TO MAMMA!!!!!!!!

Arriving at Jean Balance's office. She's the director for Hyde County School Food Service. She and her husband Leon live just down 264 toward Engelhard. They were in the process of taking two of the very nice old two story homes and combining them into one. Leon's a produce farmer with hundreds of acre's under cultivation near home and over near Nebraska, a little community on the sound near Gull Rock. All very close by. He raises mostly root vegetables year round. The soil's very rich and all the land has to be laced with canals and ditches to get rid of the excess water. Lake Mattamuskeet's close by down at New Holland. In the early teens and twenties, millions of dollars were spent to drain and cultivate it, and a canal was dug all the way to the sound. That bankrupted quite a few people and corporations. Now its a Federal Game Reserve. The thousands of ducks and geese like it that way, thank you. Its quite a site during migration when there are thousands upon thousands of Canadian and Snow geese there.

Jean needed a serving line at O.A. Peay School. We rode over just in time to see the lunch lines at their peak. She sure needed a serving line. Between breaks, I took measurements and told her I 'd get something to her in a few days.

I took the shortcut down 99 to 32 and on to Plymouth. I enjoyed that route because it took me through the Ponser community and by the Mennonite communities. It was easy to know when you entered their area. No TV antennas anywhere and everything was always so neat and clean. Sometimes the boys and girls would be outside near the school. All were dressed in black and white. The women were in long black dresses with white aprons and bonnets.

Ann Taft from Plymouth High School had called last week and this was my first chance to get over. She was finishing up with her reports with I walked in. her range wasn't big enough. The ovens were the biggest problem.

"Bob, I don't need all the 10 burners, just more oven space."

She had some room to spare under the hood, so I suggested replacing the range with a 6 burner/ one oven and adding a double convection oven.

"Send me some information. Something's got to be done."

On the way back down 64 to Jamesville, I'd take a short-cut over to Washington going back home, I kicked around how to price Ann's Equipment.

Totally oblivious to what was going on, I heard a siren. Looking in the rear-view mirror, it was full of FLASHING BLUE LIGHTS.

"Holy Shit!"

My heart passed my ass so fast, the draft almost took the rest of me with it. You've heard of your whole life passing before your eyes, it won't my life, it was my driving record.

"Jesus H. Christ!!!!!!!"

I'd just gotten the last ticket off my record, now this. The squelch broke on the CB.

"Hey Cousin, you got your ears on?"

Who the hell? In a great sense of despair, my turn signal on and slowing down, I keyed the mike.

"This is the Country Cousin."

No CB lingo here. Just utter despair.

"This is the Cigar Smoker, I got your back door. 10-4?"

Walter Parrish!! Damn his hide. He'd just cost my 10 years of my life. He pulled up along side. I'd never seen him laugh so hard. He shook his finger at me and pulled away.

"Cigar Smoker got your front door now Cousin, put the hammer down and bring her on." I planned to take the short-cut, but looking at my watch, I knew it was break-time for him. I rolled the windows down to get the smell out and followed him to the Town and Country. The guys at the "Family Table" would enjoy this. I rode the "Rocking Chair back to Greenville via 903. Sunshine was on the "front door" and Moonbeam was on the back. I caught Candy Man passing through and told him I'd be back tomorrow to stay over. Ending up in the "DuPont" shift change traffic, I knew getting home would be slow. The Trucker's were on channel 1-9 now. They'd moved because of all the bleed-over on nine. South of K-town I switched over to 1-4.

"Breaker 1-4, Cousin on the side."

"KBM-8355, Cousin, where are you?"

"Just north of the Sandy Bottom cut-off."

"Can you come by?"

"10-4."

"KBM-8355 clear."

There was something wrong.

"KJR- 4734 clear."

When I walked in, Joe was standing there. He didn't look comfortable at all. I asked him what was wrong.

"Bob, the man's in town."

"You mean the Friendly Candy Company?"

"Yeah, the FCC."

"Where, who's seen him?"

"Been spotted in Kinston."

"What does he look like?"

"On a green station wagon, all sorts of antenna's all over it. The one in the middle turns. That's the one he finds you with.

One thing the FCC had going for them. Somehow they'd instilled a fear into CB'ers that was phenomenal. All anyone had to do was mention them and everybody would shut down. You wouldn't hear a station with a booster for days, weeks sometimes. There was a guy around Kinston, who's handle was "Cosmo". Something about him reeked with "FCC". Nobody trusted him and would leave the channel when he came on. He'd been real active the past several weeks. He always wanted to know everything about your set-up. Everybody else was interested too. But not like him.

I looked at Joe.

"Rainbow Fertilizer?"

Yeah, we really need to get the word out.

Some months ago at a get-to-gather at Green Six's we'd formulated a plan to let everyone know when the "Man" was in town. It would be "Rainbow Fertilizer". That would be easy enough to talk about over the air and no one would suspect what we were talking about.

Standing in the shack when I got home, I tried to decide what to do. obviously, Charlie had to take a vacation. Guess I'd pull the Cobra 139 out of Moth Balls. It was after six before I had a "Respectable Shack". I wouldn't be able to get out of my underwear, But!, I was legal. The CB shop was another matter. After stashing the illegal goodies in the "packhouse" I took another look just to be sure. A pickup pulled up outside. It was Monkey Wrench.

"Cous., how you doing?"

"Little shook up right now."

"What's wrong Cous.?"

"Man's in town."

"Man! Rainbow Fertilizer Man?"

"That Man."

"Damn Cous. When'd you find out?"

"This afternoon, Insurance Man told me."

"That's why its so quite on the channels."

"Probably, word spread like wildfire."

"That Cosmo have anything to do with it."

Boy, you could see those wheels turning. They'd lynch him if he was. Slick came by looking for a microphone.

"You mean he's here, in Kinston?"

I told him what the Insurance Man had said. He guessed we'd all better lay low for awhile. The landline rung. Green Six was livid.

"I told you boys what was going to happen. He's gonna get all of us. We'd all be in jail before the week's out.

"My mess is for sale!" Anybody want it can come get it!"

There was no calming Six down. I hung up and it rung again. Cricket, down Beulaville way bringing me the news. Nobody was using the rigs. It was dead quite. Crackerjack came over and joined in the "wake". Guy from Chinquapin had just pulled up wanting a radio. When he heard what was happening, said he'd come back later. Monkey Wrench left to tell Grandma not to use the kicker and let his youngun's all know. Del called on the intercom and said supper was ready. Slick and Crackerjack left, I closed up and walked to the house.

"Don't guess there'll be much business for a few days, Man's in town."

"Man, what man?"

"You remember that meeting we went to over at Green Sixes couple of months ago?"

"Yes, why?"

"We talked about the FCC man and what we were going to do it he came."

"Uh huh."

"He's here."

"What are you going to do?"

"I don't know, lay low I guess."

"Is he going to get you into any trouble?"

"Not if I can help it."

Now right in the midst of this mess I gotta tell you about "Miss Del's, the Lady's" cornbread. If there was a little sunshine in my life right at this moment, it was her cornbread. I'd watched her throw it together a thousand times and it always came out the same. She baked it in the oven on her special cornbread pan and it came out wonderfully thin, crispy and absolutely delicious. Since our divorce there have been many times when I'd just crave it. Along with her collards and fatback meat.........God! It was heaven.

"Hey Miss Del. Send me some cornbread please!"

After supper I walked back to the shop. Sat around for a little while and went back to the shack. The channels were all but dead. The locals had gone into "hiding". There was a little skip coming in from Missouri. Nobody was touching it. Nobody! I turned it off and tried copying some code on the receiver Don had loaned me. It was an old tube type and floated badly. 20 meters was wide open and the Novice portion was hopping. I copied there to get warmed up, then slipped up into the general portion. Jumping from 5 words a minute to 13+ would work on you. I scribbled several pages of mostly incoherent characters. I'd get 3 or 4 words then miss a bunch. I eased up into the extra class section. They were flying. 20+ WPM. Now folks, that's hauling ass. I could pick out a word here and there. I was told you had to stop listening for the individual letters and start hearing complete words. Won't no danger of me doing that any time soon. One thing, the receiver kept floating and you had to continually zero beat it in to copy. Several hours of that would have you climbing the walls. Thats why the latest American Express Mini Catalog caught me. There was a Sony; CRF 320 staring back at me. "Solid State" full coverage 500 hz. Through 30 Mhz. Plus standard AM and FM broadcast. Digital read-out, noise blankers, automatic gain control, antenna tuning, built-in FM antenna and broadband antenna plus external connections. That thing was beautiful and only $1,895.00. Now Good Buddy, that's a bunch of Green Stamps but with American Expresses "Easy Payments" and no interest…..

"Hello American Express. Send me your item number……..

Five days later, she was here. "Beautiful!" The most stable rig I've ever seen. Copying code was a thousand percent easier. I still love listening to it today. Expensive, but really an excellent investment.

Next morning I loaded up early and headed off to Scotland Neck. That turned out to be a bum lead so I called on the Idle Hour Restaurant and drove up just north of town to Braddy's Barbecue. If it had been Monday, I wouldn't have gotten within a hundred miles of it. Monday was "Chitlin day" Okay, I grew up on a farm, love pork and ham, but Chitterlings are not for me. Anything that smelled like that couldn't be good.

"Hey Bob, we looked for you yesterday. Where were you?"

"Mr. Braddy, it just couldn't be helped or I'd have been here."

He laughed and gave me an order for some smallwares."

I left and headed up 258 for Rich Square. After calling on a nursing home and the Quaker House Restaurant, I put her in the wind toward Greenville, I barely slowed down passing through Roxobel and Kelford. Perdue hadn't arrived yet so I had the hammer down on 308. You had to slow down in Lewiston, even if you took the back way through Woodsville. When I pulled out on Hwy. 11, an eighteen wheeler passing northbound gave the T-Bird wid all dem antennas a holler.

"10-4 Hot Rod, preciate that smokey report. Country Cousin be doing it thisa way."

"Hold dat hammer down Cousin, she's all yours. Hot Rod be rollin north."

I had her in the wind when I crossed the river bridge. Didn't take long to get to Oak City. Got another Smokey Report there and put the pedal to the metal. Caught the light at Bethel and fired her up again.

"How bout you southbound. Got your ears on?"

"10-4, You got the Country Cousin. Go ahead."

"Gearjammer back to ya, Cousin. Dem antennas work fer ya?"

"10-4 Gearjammer, gottem just right."

"10-4, I gotta git me some. You got a county mountie southbound bout 5 miles back. Other'ern that, she be clean and green."

"10-4 Gearjammer, you're clean all the way to Lewiston. Let her go."

"7-3's Gearjammer gone."

I stopped by the Ramada and told Candy Man I'd forgot I had school on Tuesday, I 'd see him next week

"Golly, you know I didn't want to miss the "Colpitt's and Hartley oscillators."

After class I stopped by Joe's to see what was going on. He had heard about the station wagon being all over the county. He sure would be glad when he was gone. I drove home, had a late supper, copied some more code and called it a day.

170

Wednesday I had breakfast with Sugar Bear at Kings. Victor was all over us.

"Boy's, you know the man's in town. I took all my mess to the beach. He ain't going to catch me with anything."

Mike didn't believe the man was really in town. I was beginning to wonder. If he was really around, why hadn't someone been arrested? We laughed about it a little even though I still wasn't sure. The local's had completely stopped talking. You didn't even hear "Sugar Britches" down around LaGrange carrying on with the truckers. It was kinda weird. I drove back over to Washington and met with Kay. Her dishwasher booster was bad and it was going to take a week for one to come from Atlanta. She ordered it and we visited 3 other schools. Then we had lunch at the Holiday Inn. The owner, Ken Phillips, came over a griped about something we'd sent him. I came back after lunch and picked it up for credit. Everybody knew Ken hated restaurants and only had this one because Holiday Inn required it. Later when his son, Kirk, took over, he was exactly the same way. Some years later, Kirk's group had acquired the Holiday Inn property in Kinston. As usual he was at war with the local Health Inspector. He'd assured her that there was no funds available to upgrade the kitchen. The very next week, posted on the sign out front for God and everyone to see. "Just completed, million dollar room renovation." The Health Lady came in the next morning during breakfast and "pad-locked" the restaurant. The seated customers were not allowed to finish their meals. Kirk was "IN THE TREES". The food manager called and asked if I'd come down. After looking over the needs and the items they'd been gigged on, a plan to get re-opened was divised. He begged me to get Kirk out of there before he had a heart attack. I took him to several towns and wasted a day. After finally calming him down, I explained what was taking place back on the property. After dinner at the Country Squire in Kenansville and getting Kirk drunk enough, I took him back. The clean-up lasted all night and the next day. Replacement of pieces that couldn't be cleaned brought a return inspection the next day and reopening on the following day. You don't shove crap in the inspector's faces.

The Four Leaf Clover perked my day up on the way back to Kinston. She had a very sexy voice and could really carry a conversation. We were on 102 heading west toward Ayden. I usually took the shortcut at Stokestown crossroads, but today, I went all the way to Ayden. I signed with her, no, we didn't eyeball, come on! and turned south on 11.

The Rug Rat gave a clean report back toward K-Town. I brought her on in.

Next morning I was out again early. Absolutely nothing was going on locally. Passing through Ayden I gave Little Cricket a call.

"Break Eight, how about you Little Cricket? You around?"

"Go ahead Traveling Man, you're kinda weak, but I still copy."

Yeah, Yeah, my Scorpion was on vacation, outta the county.

"Where's Flyrod?"

"Somewhere between Snow Hill and Goldsboro."

"Can you hit him?"

"10-4."

"Tell him the man's in "K-Town. 10-4?"

"10-4! Think I heard something about that. I'll swing the beam down his way now. Thanks, have a good morning, Little Cricket clear."

"73's Little Cricket, Traveling Man clear."

"Break eight for the Flyrod. Little Cricket's trying."

Trying hell, she had that MoonRaker 4 pointed right over my head plus whatever else she needed.

"Go ahead Little Cricket, Flyrod got ya."

"10-4, where are you going when you leave Goldsboro?"

"Over to "K-Town. 10-4?"

"10-4, thought so, I just talked to Traveling Man. He said the Man's in town. 10-4?"

"10-4, tell him good morning and preciate it."

"10-4, see you after a while."

"Flyrod clear."

I didn't miss a word. Flyrod was 10-8 wherever he was.

"Hey Traveling Man. Did you copy Flyrod?"

She had cranked back down and gone to the ground plane.

"10-4 Little Cricket. Talk to you two later. Have a good day."

I 20-27ed back to the trucker's channel. Somebody was breaking for a 10-36. Sounded normal. Just rolling into Greenville. Triple Nickel came on the channel, blowing smoke as usual. He'd sit there for hours passing out info to the truckers and chewing the rag.

"Morning Triple Nickel. How'er you doing?"

"10-8 and 10-10 Traveling Man, how bout you?"

"10-8, Triple Nickel, looks like a great day. Catcha later."

"10-40-Roger-4 Traveling Man. Keep it between the ditches. Triple Nickel by."

I'd just arrived at the Holiday Inn. Time for coffee with the boys.

Arriving in "University City" anymore was beginning to be a hassle. Greenville's been growing by leaps and bounds for at least 10 years. A person couldn't live here very long without being swept up in "Pirate Mania". Football fever was everywhere led by some very dynamic people like Les Garner and Joe Hallow. If you ever have the opportunity, have Joe bestow one of those special Lebanese Prayers on you. I promise it will cure all your ills. Joe's the "Blue Ribbon" distributor here. It the prayer don't work, a six pak will. Joe reached financial bliss when Lynn Stensen opened the Rathskeller on 5th street in the late sixties. It was followed by the Elbow Room, Attic and Bob Saad's "Fiddler's Three". The Pirate Club was strong and full of energetic people. The Medical School was coming, thanks to Dr. Leo Jenkins. What a man. Everything about Greenville was exploding with development. Thanks to Country Commissioner's like Mr. Bruce Strickland, Greenville and Pitt County had picked up the ball when other towns in the area seemed to have dropped it. not only did they pick it up, they ran with it. Industries were popping up everywhere you looked. Burroughs Wellcome, Eaton Corporation, Proctor and Gamble, Grady, White Boats, just to mention a few. Industry had finally discovered the last great frontier.

"Morning Becky, Miss Ethel, good morning Gladys."

"Well sir, you made it."

"Good morning Mr. Clinker."

Nat Van Nortwick would come by most mornings and have coffee. Living in Greenville, he travels about the same area I do for Cherokee Brick Co. He's been peddling bricks for several years. Hence the handle "Clinker". We kicked around some of the more important things going on in the world, fishing, weather, the body in that sexy bikini out by the pool, and of course, CB. By then, Rev. Willis Wilson, pastor of Reedy Branch FWB Church and quite an "after dinner speaker" (The Squire of Reedy Branch) joined us. He knows more jokes, clean ones or course, and how to tell them, than anyone I know.

"Gentlemen, have you heard the one about the drunk sitting in the bar. He turned to the guy on his right, Buddy, did you spill a drink on me? No sir, not me. He turns to the guy sitting on his left. Mister, did you spill a drink on me? Not me. Looking down, well, it musta been an inside job!"

Two cups of coffee with Willis, and your sides hurt for the rest of the day.

"Morning Mr. Country Cou-sin."

Now that drawl couldn't belong to anyone but, "Four J's" , its going to be a long morning.

"Come on in and join the crowd."

In walked "Sugar Foot", Lord God, L.G. Deyton. Now it's complete. Willis looked over at Joel,

"Joel, did you notice the new personalized plates on my car?"

"No, Willis, musta missed it."

"Yeah they finally came in. They fit me perfectly."

Nothing would do but we all walk out front.

"FAP 6963"

"Yes gentlemen, that stands for "Fat and Pretty". Thats what I tell the ladies in my congregation. It really stands for "Fat Ass Preacher.""

We all had a big laugh and went back inside. Fourteen cups of coffee and three trips to the "Wee Wee Machine" later, the group broke up.

I'd already missed three appointments and had to go to work.

"Becky, may I have a landline please. Donna, I'm running late, can I see you after lunch? 2 will be fine. Thanks Becky, see you later."

"Breaker 1-0 for the Traveling Man."

"Go ahead Clinker."

"Traveling Man, forgot to ask, you going to be around for coffee in the morning?"

"10-4, got to go by the store first, be a little later."

"10-4, see you then. Clinker clear."

"Hey Traveling Man, that was some cup of coffee, two hours, man, you ain't right!"

"You got that right Triple Nickel."

"Okay, 73's, Triple Nickel Clear."

I knew Walter Brooks would be standing on his head when I got over to the hospital. Something had happened to one of the fryers and he'd left a message for me to get in touch,

"NOW!!!!!".

I'd called and left a message with Nancy I'd be there this morning and morning was disappearing fast. Finding a parking place at Pitt County Memorial Hospital (PCMH) was getting to be a real problem. Every time they'd designate a parking area for the Vendors, they'd take it away and build something on it. I'd asked Mr. Bruce Strickland what the projected finish date for the complex was and he informed me that it never would be completed. I drove around and around finally parking somewhere I shouldn't and walked down the long, long hall, how long?, long enough they were using tricycles to get from one end to the other. Nancy looked up.

" Hey, you made it. You really don't want to see him. He's having a bad hair day."

I sure knew what that meant. Walt was special, but you had to understand him. Most of the time he was affectionately referred to as "Papa Smurf". The full beard alluded to that along with his pleasant demeanor. Those other times he was something like the "Wild Man from Borneo" Having been in the Navy, he had that special way with words. He never had to be asked twice what the problem was. You'd get it the first time.

From down the hall, I heard him.

Nancy, you're right. I don't want to see him. I turned to leave and there he stood.

"What the Hell took you so damn long? If I'd had a PO, you'd broke the doors down."

"Hell Walt, I got here as fast as I could. What's the problem?"

"God Damn Fryer blew up. Damn near burnt the place down."

He led me down the corridor to his shop, (and office til they finally moved him to the third floor away from all the activity (the "IVORY TOWER"). He's been quiet as a kitten every since. OK, almost.) There was no question about the fryer having a problem. It had definitely been in a fire.

"Damn thing created havoc the other day. The Exhaust Hood Fire Protection System went off and it took hours to clean up the mess."

I certainly knew what he meant by that. Several years before, something had set the system off at the Town & Country Restaurant in Williamston just before the noon meal covering all the food with powder. Everything had to be thrown away. Needless to say, that was a very costly experience. Possibly the only good thing that came out of it was my being able to pick up a few choice words and phrases that had eluded me up to that point. I felt my vocabulary was complete afterwards .

"So what can I do to help?"

Walt told me he thought the high limit thermostat hung and the fryer got hotter and hotter until it ignited. He wanted someone to come down and confirm or deny that observation. The fryer was part of the new kitchen package that had been furnished by the Contract Division of my company and I could feel the weight of that monkey crawling on Montgomery Green's back. I told Walt I'd be in touch.

Stopping at the Three Steers Restaurant, I called Bill Misner and filled him in on the problem. He assured me that that if anybody had a problem, it would be the manufacturer, not us.

"Bob, you in town tonight?"

Woody was trying to line up a drinking buddy for the evening.

"Naw, heading in shortly."

"Let's have a couple before you go."

"Sounds good to me Woody, bring em on."

"Faye, bring a couple of beers."

After the forth one, I headed out. Usually I could hold four til I got home. If I had five or more, there'd be a plumbing problem between DuPont and Kinston and disposal facilities were non-existent there except for a couple of woods paths. "Hey, when the bucket's full and the water's still coming, anywhere will work. Reminds me of the time some years later when we had a camper parked in Holiday Travel Park at Emerald Isle, NC. We'd spend every weekend from March through November there. We'd met Flynn and Glenda Hardee there and had become good friends. Flynn and I spent most of the time consuming large quantities of beer either laying on the beach watching the clouds, OK, girls go by or someone surfcasting. The girls of course were much more interesting. Sometimes we'd take his Cherokee on the beach, park, cast out our empty lines, hell, you didn't want some lousy old fish to bite and get in the way of our drinking, sit back and enjoy. The wee-wee machine wasn't a problem, just walk out into the surf and dump or open the Cherokee door and stand there with your head down as if you were having your daily prayer. The evenings always brought cookouts. Seafood and steak were always on the top of the list with the beer topping Flynn's and mine. Their two daughters were always on the run, grabbing something from the picnic table, they'd be gone. When Del and I first moved into the park, we bought Spence and Donna's camper. They'd purchased a new 38 foot Aluma-lite and Popeye had moved the Holiday Rambler across the park to our location. Both sides of the park were lined with "permanent spots" except down at the "Gazebo", the entrance to the beach. There was lots and lots of steps leading up to the top of the sand dune and the Gazebo was on top. More steps led down to the beach. Standing in the Gazebo was magnificent. Looking to the right toward the point was just unforgettable. The point was around 4 miles away and in the early eighties, there were plenty of undeveloped stretches of dunes. Of course it was dotted with different subdivisions. The exclusive one being "Land's End." Ronnie Watson, owner of the Holiday Trav-L Park also owned properties, including Land's End, all over Emerald Isle and Cape Carteret. One of my favorite activies was to walk down the beach toward the point passing Ronnie's home on the corner of Land's End and then crossing the dunes and visiting the many homes under construction. Houses in the first two rows began above a half million with the lots above $165,000.00. Many times we'd ride up Coast Guard Road to the Land's End entrance. Being gated and staffed with a guard, you just didn't drive in. Most of the time, there'd be an open house and that would be our ticket in. we visited one home almost completed that had a third floor master "Hot Tub" that was unbelievable. The sunken tub in the middle of the room was surrounded by marble with a built in bar. all four sides were "one sided' dark glass affording views I couldn't believe. Standing there, my mind did the rest.

"Wow, get me outta here."

I couldn't have afforded the bathroom fixtures. A lot of years ago around 1970 or 71, I got a to call Maynard Hicks at Emerald Isle. If I'd ever been there, I couldn't remember it. Being almost totally inaccessible for years, only by ferry from Swansboro or four-wheeler from Salter Path, the sleepy little fishing village awoke with the arrival of Bill McLean, Maynard Hicks and Bill Spell.

They purchased large portions of property and began making plans to market it. Politically in touch, by hook or crook, they finally succeeded in getting a paved road from Salter Path. The agreement being reached just two days before the Gubernatorial elections that year. That brought a trickle of investors and prospective home owners. Although mostly, it brought folks looking for a place to build a fishing shack or a place to park a camper or trailer. That not what these gentlemen were looking for. They needed a bridge. They tried every way possible to get someone in Raleigh to listen. All attempts fell on deaf ears. Their local political clout meant nothing in the Capitol City. They needed a big hitter. As they tell the story, that big hitter turned out to be the Holden Brothers or First Citizens Bank and Trust Company. These gentlemen had clout, bunches of it. A deal was struck selling them one third of the property owned by the group at a greatly reduced price, they used the term; gave it away. In turn the Holden's would lobby for a high rise bridge spanning Bogue Sound from Cape Carteret to just below the little village, maybe a mile from the ferry terminal. That's where I came in. They now had traffic and no place to stay. Construction had already begun on the Islander Motel when I arrived, in fact the rooms were almost ready for occupancy. They kept running into the building inspector because of the unapproved building methods they were employing. As I recall, they were acting as building contractor themselves. This project belonged to Bill McLean and Maynard. Each night would bring out the juice and that would begin their planning session. They described what they had in mind for a restaurant and lounge and gave me a set of blueprints. As usual, the area dedicated to the restaurant and lounge were blank. Companies like ours were expected to do a layout and in return get the order. Next day, I drove to Raleigh and met with Bill Misner. He said he'd take it from there and I could work on the smallwares package. Bill called a week or so later saying he was ready. I made an appointment for the next day. Bill flew down and picked me up at Stalling's Field in Kinston. We landed on the ninth fairway at Star Hill Country Club. Maynard picked us up and we drove over to the site. Bill had done an excellent job and the proposal was accepted. I'd do the smallwares presentation later.

The Islander Motel, Restaurant and Lounge opened in 1972 and was a huge success. Maynard asked if we'd be interested in taking payment for any part of the package in beach front property. We laughed, what in the world did we want with sand. The lots down at the point beside the Coast Guard Station were going in the $12,000.00 dollar range then. In the eighties, the same lots were going for $150,000.00 plus range and now in the nineties, I can't count that high. What can I say, apparently I'm a very astute business man. Ha!

One Sunday I felt totally bloated and couldn't stop complaining. Glenda offered me a fluid pill for relief, warning me not to take it until I got home. I promised, walked inside the camper and gulped it down. Del had finished loading her car and she and Windi took off. I rolled the canopy up, turned the water off, checked the lights and air. Time to go. It had begun to rain making departure that much more aggravating. Between the hours of 11 AM and 6 PM 99% of the weekend beachgoers would head back home creating a massive traffic jam between Emerald Isle and Kinston. This day was no exception. I finally pulled in line crossing the high rise bridge over Bogue sound and started up Hwy. 58. The normal 20 minute ride to Maysville was becoming a 40 minute one.

"Knock, Knock!"

My bladder was calling.

"Damn, what was happening?"

My bucket was running over and wanted to be emptied NOW! If I could just make it to Maysville. No, dammit, NOW! I eased the van onto the shoulder. What was I going to do? The traffic was bumper to bumper. I finally found a milkshake cup. There I was, kneeling down, filling the cup, dumping it out the sliding door, filling it again. The same thing happened two more times before I could get home. Next time Glenda said wait. I'd wait.

After my separation, I met Pat, "Whag". Whag? Oh yes, Wild, Hot and Good!!!!!!!. Hell no, I didn't tell her mother what the letters meant. Just a nickname Lucille. Like your's, the Kentucky Fried Queen. We're all pretty sure where that came from (I'll share that story with you later). All the activity kept the fluids worked off. No, you figure it out. I ain't going there.

I certainly was in no hurry, hell, couldn't do anything but look at the radio when I got home.

What was this? The channels were busy again.

"Break 1-4. Insurance Man, you around?"

"10-4 Cousin, bring it on back."

"What's going on, Sounds like normal again."

"That's a big 10-4, Man's in Jacksonville now."

When I got home, Del said the phone had been ringing off the hook. Call Green Six first.

The first thing was the plumbing problem, then I'd call Six. As they say,

"Relief is just a bathroom away."

"Miss Hazel, Six around?"

"Sure is Traveling Man, uh, Bearded Man ah……….."

I had so many handles, nobody knew what to call me.

"Hey Bearded Man, how you doing?"

"Fine Six, how bout you?"

"Not so good Bearded Man, this thing about the man's got me tore all to pieces."

"Aw, don't worry bout him Six, he's gone now."

"Well, maybe that's true, but, well anyway, I asked a few of the fellers to come over tonight for cake and coffee and I want you to come."

"Okay Six, what time?"

"Anytime after seven. Bring the Lady too."

"Okay, see you then."

Six was all shook up to say the least. Bo had called and asked if we were going, so we went together. When we arrived, the yard was full of cars. Inside the same thing. Let's see, Insurance man, Woodpecker, Monkey Wrench, Blue Dragon, Big Red, Night Hawk, Bull Dozier, Carolina Max, Girl Watcher and Hammer Head, the room was full. Miss Hazel and all the gals were up front. Six brought in more chairs. Crackerjack and I were introduced around. Eyeballing each other for the first time was always interesting.

'Fellers, you all know why I called you. We gotta do something bout knowing when the man's around. Rainbow Fertilizer ain't working. Nobody's on the air when he's around. Six was right. Everybody just clammed up.

Had anybody seen him. Several had talked to somebody that had. Joe had already told me. Somebody had slipped up to the Van,(Van, I thought it was a station wagon.) peeped inside, wall to wall electronic gear. Outside covered with antennas. That direction finder in the center. It had to be him. Okay if it was him. How were you going to know he was coming. It would be no different than right now. Everybody in a hundred miles knew he was in Kinston. He'd be in their backyard next (Much later I found out that the FCC was grossly understaffed with just 2 agents in the entire southeast responsible for the bands and we were just a very small portion of their responsibility. If a station wasn't really causing big problems interfering with the police, firemen, hospitals or other public service agencies or maybe wiping out half a town's ability to watch TV. They didn't have the time or personal to be bothered.). The best thing they had going for them was exactly what was happening. As long as they had that. They didn't need agents. We were self-governing, so to speak. Same thing with the Smokey's. Long as they had the CBer's, we'd do their job for them. All they had to do was make an appearance, then go back home or to their favorite "Coffee Place" and sit back. The smokey reports would be flying for at least two hours on each siting.

We really won't getting anywhere. Six was too shook to hear anything but doom.

"Fellers, that man's gonna walk in here one day and take everything I've got. I'm gittin out while I can."

That caused an uproar. We were all trying to calm Six down. Insurance Man did finally get him to listen to reason. It took a lot of persuading to get him to understand the he didn't need those "Beams". Six had been on the air over a year without them and really talked to everyone he wanted to.

"Okay Fellers, I'll stay on. BAREFOOTED THOUGH!!!!!!"

Later I bought the "Set of Beams" and sold them to someone as eager as I had once been looking for that first "Box".

After Six calmed down, a good time was had by all. The fellowship was special among CBer's. The get-to-gether broke up around 10. On the way home it suddenly dawned on me that the Man was gone.

"Hello Skipland, Skipland, Skipland."

It took the better part of 3 hours to get back "10-8" on the base and mobile. It was well after 1AM when I cranked Charlie Back up. The band was still open. I worked the following on AM.

"Silver Fox	Nova Scotia"
"Red Rooster	Nova Scotia"
"Little Wad	Mass."
"Mr. Mo	Mass."
"Hot Rod	Nova Scotia"
"W.B.	Nova Scotia"
"Captain Kidd	Nova Scotia"
"The 466	Mass."
"Seagull	New Jersey"
"Skipper Number 2	Montreal"
"Crazy Horse	Montreal"

It was 3 AM. Time to go to bed.

"Where to next?"

Between the Skip, School, the CB Shop…..oh, and my regular job. They were killing me. Oh, what a way to go. I was learning just enough in school and messing in the shop to be able to "turn the rigs up"…okay the solid state's didn't turn up much. Unlike their older brother's with the tubes, it was rare to get more than 5 or 6 watts out of them. Mostly it was more like 4 ½ watts. The modulation was more important anyway. Getting good modulation gave you a great station. Too much modulation splattered you all over the band. That's what the "Power Mikes" did. Weren't their faults. We'd turn that little knob as far up as it would go.

"How's it sound now?"

Hell, it probably sounded good. More likely fuzzy because of over-modulation. It would be "Grumbling and Muttering" 3 or 4 channels on each side of the one you were on. I guess that was part of the fun though. That's why Citizen Bander's won't allowed more than 4 watts. We didn't have to know what we were doing. When the 40 channel rigs showed up in "76", everything I 'd ever learned was trashed. They did nothing like the 23's. the modulation and output were easy to max out. Changing or adding more channels was very different because the radio's used different methods to come up with the channels. I'd gotten good at adding "little boxes" on the older ones. That would have to change.

More and more, I spent my time on Sideband. Without the carrier, talking was much simpler and the signals just went further.

Mostly if you were on the "Upper Channels" they liked to call them "Frequencies", you could only get a QSO on sideband. No one was on the Ancient Mary side up there. All those technical folks I'd run into earlier were much easier to talk to since I'd started school and studying to become a Ham. Lots of times the late night QSO's would run for what seemed to be hours. There was the opportunity to really get inside each-other's shacks and be completely familiar with the equipment and what was more fun, understand how it got there. Very few of us started with the "Right Stuff". Mostly we'd copy the friend's setup that introduced us. The Ham's called those guys, "Elmer's". The tinkering and experimenting was especially prevalent on sideband. It was very easy to get into a conversation with someone that was talking way over your head. I guess that's what intrigued me most. There were many times when I'd stop at Southeastern or Pair Electronics looking for information concerning something I'd heard or talked about the preceding night. Both places had books available on radio theory, kit building, antennas and other related subjects. There'd be many electronics classes that would turn into CB related discussions. Mr. Civils would let it continue using the opportunity to mix it with class related subjects.

Using frequency counters and a "Kit built" Heathkit scope certainly helped me to service the equipment that kept popping up in my shop. I'd also installed a frequency counter in line with Charlie so I always knew where I actually was. Many times another station would mention that you were off frequency. Letting them know you were using a counter would quickly end that conversation. The scope on the other hand gave me the opportunity to show someone how their voice envelope would splatter when they over-modulated. As someone said.

"A picture's worth a thousand words."

In class and well as in the "Real World", transistors were replacing tubes, right and left. That certainly helped me. Even with class, my grasp of radio theory with tubes was grossly lacking. I cannot tell you why, but transistors seemed infinitely easier to grasp,

AND just at the moment when the fog began to clear, in came the "Thousand Legged Worms." The Integrated Chips were a wonderful innovation but they reeked havoc with the "Shade Tree Repairman" like me. Nothing was the same again. When those little boogers arrived with the 40 channel sets. My day as a CB repairman began to wane. Not only did they require different equipment, logic counters, etc. You also had to know how the use them. I focused my attention on the Output Finals and Modulation Transistors. Anything other than that would probably get your rig an "Expense Charged Vacation" back to the factory. That would take 6 to 10 weeks. Along with the 40 channels, the prices dropped to nothing. you could buy a new rig cheaper than getting it repaired. AM 40 channel rigs could be bought for fifty bucks. Not only that, they could be bought anywhere. Dime stores, Super Markets, Drug Stores, Hardware Stores and even the Country Gas Station. They were all getting in on the "Boom". Kraco's were great little AMer's Fantastic modulation, easy to turn up and set. I sold dozens of them. There were so many other brands, I completely lost count. There were still expensive ones if that was what you were looking for. Most of the New CBer's, "What do you want for Christmas?" who came on line after Christmas of 75 and 76 just wanted to be "10-8" with the crowd. That meant mobiles only. Hell, most normal people, that's what they say, don't need one at home. They had TV and even if talking on it "inside" ever came up, a $20.00 power supply and cheap ground plane was all it took. Only the serious "Jawjackers" went for the complete base station layout and then only a small percentage went over the edge like me. Reminds me of the Leisure Suits. God, I loved them. The second year they were out, everybody sold them. Seems they were extremely easy to manufacture. The powers that ruled the fashions for the coming year put an end to that. Extensive advertising and a complete cessation of manufacturing them, brought a quick end to them. Remember the digital watches. Almost over night they were raining down all over us. Everybody had them and they were cheap. Where are they now? Same problem.

Skip of course was a fun thing for a couple of years. It was reeking so much havoc on the locals, they were beginning to lose interest. The eighteen wheeler's were getting pretty tired too. They had enjoyed their immense popularity in the beginning. Now it was completely impossible to carry on a QSO with your buddy or meeting another trucker. There'd be fifty breaks everytime a mike was keyed. It would take a few more years, but they'd finally lash out and try to take their communications medium back. The one way they found that worked the best was the vulgar language. It sure ran me off. Riding by one's self was one thing, but being with mixed groups, wife, friends, etc. got the rig turned off. It's been a long time since I've tuned in. Hopefully they have their channels back. The popularity is one thing but……. Its like our Movie Stars and Singers. Once they're popular, they no longer can be with the populace without being mobbed. Guess there's a price to pay for everything.

I was still experimenting with the antennas on the tower because it was so easy to lay down, I'd change the ground plane and TV antenna above the MoonRaker real often. TV reception had really changed with the 20' Quantum Boom at 90 feet. I'd extended the mast using a 1" pipe. I, well really Del was receiving channels, 3, 4, 5, 6, 7, 9, 11, 12, 22, 28 and 40 and early in the morning channel 2 out of the Triad. Satellite TV was just around the corner and I was already talking with Joe Butts at Southeastern about it. He had already scheduled me for a "Day Class" in Kinston teaching the Theory and Installation of Channel Master Receiving Dishes. I installed the first one in the community that December. Del wanted no part of it. The way I had it setup, there were no local channels and that meant no "Day's of our lives" or "As the world Twirls". Using the dish took some getting use to. There were so many available channels on so many different satellites. Galaxy 5 was the prime one. Located 25,000 miles above the Hawaiian Islands, the dish had to be pointed just above the treeline to access it. Then every 5 degrees there was another bird. Each bird had 24 channels, excuse me, 24 "Transponders", 12 up and 12 down. Okay, Okay, 12 horizontally polarized and 12 vertically polarized. Using those polarization's allowed the maker to get 24 on each bird. The 5 degree spacing allowed dish user to lock in on that satellite only and not get "bleedover" from it's neighbor. Not all 24 channels were for public use. Mostly they were being used privately. There were many being used to send out packaged programming to TV stations to be broadcast on their regular schedules. Many times when you'd hear people talking about up-coming shows, you had already seem them and dropped little teasing tid-bits about them. Blew their minds when they'd see the show and you were correct in all aspects. Most folks thought when it was being viewed, that's when it was happening. One of the programs I especially enjoyed was the airing of Garrison Keeler's "Prairie Home Companion" although the format was being aired as a show for "Public Radio" , it was being taped. It was evident that he nor the cast were concerned about or playing to the camera. The behind the scenes look was very enjoyable. Scrambling was almost unheard of except in a few cases. One channel, Triple XXX needed to be scrambled. It was filthy. The advertisements would make a "Sailor" Blush. What was really odd, just one channel above this junk was a "Christian Broadcast Station." The Satellite directly above the receiver at 90 degrees carried a lot of ESPN, Playboy and 2 Canadian Stations. That was my favorite bird.

With the breakup of our marriage in 87. A lot of changes took place. Del had tried very hard to keep it together, I hadn't, I knew it was over. I moved out and relocated to Wil-O-Wisp apartments in Kinston leaving her the "Home Place." I'd tried to get her away from the encroaching chicken houses for years but she wouldn't budge. She'd stay and mow those 3 acres. Couple years of that and she admitted defeat. Sold the property and located in Pink Hill. Moving from 3300 square feet and 3 acres of grass to less than 1400 square feet and a very small lot, she now had a life of her own. Only then did she begin to realize what I'd tried to tell her. That property, my dream, owned us. We didn't own it.

There was lots of turmoil in my business life also. The company I'd been with for 27 years was faltering. The founder had a stroke a couple of years back. Most said it was caused by the untimely death of his son, David. He'd brought him to Raleigh from a very successful law firm he was associated with in Cleveland or Chicago. Of course he had it made but it also, for all practical purposes ended his chance to grow. Being a company lawyer for dad's business apparently was very boring. In any case, David took his own life in William B. Umstead Park and from that moment, the "Old Man" started dying. His nephew, Jeff, who was being groomed for eventual takeover wasn't ready. I'd been given the managership; of the Kinston Branch allowing Bill Dean, who'd been there 40 years to step down and get ready for retirement. He wasn't real happy about it, and still feels badly toward me. He'd hang around through the closing of the Kinston Branch and finally retire a year later. He was the last one to get any type of retirement from the failing company. The rest of the over 200 employees were thrown away little by little. I left in 88 and went through a series of jobs looking for something I could buy, I finally formed Patrisco, Inc. in 89 and began on my own. Wish I'd done that 10 years earlier. Yeah, yeah, hindsight ain't worth a dime!

Being in Wil-O-Wisp, then in Tree Tops in Winterville, then back to Kinston in Hertiage Courts on Doctor's Row effectively ended my operations in any kind of communications. Not until I purchased a home in Woods View Subdivision just outside Kinston and now my present home in Gatewood Subdivison near Winterville, have I had the opportunity to have an outside antenna.

Closing in on Sunspot Cycle 23 due to peak in the fall of 2000 is stirring something inside of me. I find each issue of QST tugging at me. The ads create havoc with my insides. I guess, like most of us, we want to return to some portion of the past. Occasionally I look back at those trips Jim and Linda Bundy, Del, the dogs and I would make to the Blue Ridge Mountains just outside Boone. We'd rent a cabin from Pat Grady, remember her? That sexy lady at Montgomery Green. Jim and I would make sure there was a VHF contest under way. We'd set up a small 3 element beam using the porch column for support and manually rotate it. We had a commanding view of Grandfather Mountain in the distance with Roan Mountain beyond. That gave us an open door northwest. We had a ball. Always making all the contacts we could handle. It was tiring but the fun certainly overcame that. The girls just enjoyed that mountain air and spent most of their time reading or cross-stitching. Windi and Randi just slept. The cabin has long since been sold and the trips we make up that way now are no longer looking for DX. Pat and I spend most of our time in the Blowing Rock and the Little Switzerland area. No radios, just Mountain Air. Last fall we were in Blowing Rock staying at the Chetola Resort. It's one of the most beautiful settings there. Sitting on the room balcony overlooking the lake offers a wonderful opportunity just to relax. The quietness and stillness broken only by the quacking of the many ducks and geese on the lake affords the opportunity to test the backs of your eyelids. We rode over the Grandfather Mountain via the very crooked and just a scenic Hwy. 221, being one of the first visitors that day. The first stop naturally was all the way on top. After walking through the visitor's center and looking at the memorabilia, we walked out to the swinging bridge. Pat stopped just short of getting on it, suggesting I have a nice walk. Admittedly, standing there in the quite almost stopped me too. It had been over forty years since I'd stood there looking down. There was no one else on the bridge. Timidly I finally took the first steps and moved very slowly across. About half way I stopped, looked down, that wasn't a good idea, then all around. Finally reaching the other side, I paused. My mind raced back through time to the seventies. If I'd had an antenna up here, I'd been able to talk a thousand miles without skip and with the skip, it would have been wild. After becoming a ham and settling on six meters as my band of choice. Jim Bundy and I made our first trip up to Pat's cabin to participate in the June VHF contest. (I'll touch on that a bit later.) Along with the girls we rode up the parkway toward Glendale Springs to visit K4ROM, Chuck Kline. Retired manager of the DuPont Plant in Kinston, Chuck and his wife had built their retirement home just off the Blue Ridge Parkway, maybe a couple hundred yards. The view was magnificent. Everything was designed to blend in with the surroundings. I never had to wander again why he could be heard anytime back down in the flatlands. Six meters was almost high enough in the spectrum to be "line of sight". Other than Chuck, any contact beyond WA4GBE, Harold in Raleigh was stretching it. Almost every Sunday on the net, Chuck would have check-ins from three or four states. Obviously, nobody else was hearing anything. We would all secretly admire and long for a location like that.

Cell Phones have become the communications equipment of choice. No longer can you holler for a break. You certainly are much surer of your intended receiver, but the fun's no longer there. With everyone from the old school sitting back knowing that the upcoming Sunspot Cycle "Ain't going to bother them had better take another look. Between Cycle 23 and Y2K, we may be in for much more than we're aware of. Dependency on the earth orbiting satellites and electronic communications, land lines and cell phones. Cell phones, mobile phones? I got to share this one with you. Back in 1975 the mobile phone systems offered were very different then than now. I felt I needed that convenience even though my company refused to help defray the expenses. A local company in Kinston had just what I needed. Their antenna (repeater) was located up high on the WITN "High and Mighty" tower. Their coverage was immense encompassing 90 percent of my territory. I could hit the repeater from Tarboro, Oak City, Williamston, Plymouth, Swan Quarter, Belhaven, Oriental, Morehead City, Jacksonville, Kenansville, Warsaw, Goldsboro Smithfield and Kenly. Sitting on top of the high rise bridges on the Outer Banks also gave me coverage. Along with that, an answering service was included. I'd taken the option of having my horn wired to it. After running down four flights of steps from Donna Ware's office to answer it, I ended that crap and let Peggy answer it and I'd respond to the blinking light at my convenience. Besides, it would probably be the office and I didn't return their calls anyway. Damn Cheapskates.

I had just gotten the installation the day before and was returning home from Greenville. Just ahead of the DuPont shift change, I was barreling down 11 when the phone rang. At that very moment, the Radar Detector went crazy. The lights were flashing, buzzer screaming, I threw the phone in the floor and stood the T-Bird on her nose. At last glance before the brakes. "75MPH". My heart back in my chest, still pumping hard, I eased off the side of the road. Everything in the car was now in front of me in the floor or plastered against the windshield on the dash. I still hadn't seen Smokey. It took several minutes to figure out what had happened. The phone's close proximity and probably 3rd, 4th. Or 5th. harmonics had set the detector off. You can bet your "come-to-gethers" that didn't happen again.

The predictions are staggering. This is predicted to be one of the 2 biggest Cycles since records have been kept. That goes back a long, long way, 1755. Not since that time have we been so dependent on communications that can be drastically affected by the solar storms. Those solar storms are the meat of fantastic communications in the VHF and UHF Ham bands. 6 meters and above will be, as they say, Wide Open. One man's tragedy is another man's opportunity. Should I, or shouldn't I............, I probably will. It's tugging very hard. I don't really know which way to turn. I could do it all via the computer......Computer? Now Good Buddy, I'll tell you one thing. That's the hardest chunk I've ever tried to chew. In 1990 I'd just started my new business and it was becoming very apparent that I needed help with the books. As had been proved many, many times over the years, books and numbers ain't my thing. I learned how to handle the checking account. I'd just keep throwing extra money into it staving off that eventual call from the bank telling me I'd better "do something." Then? I'd throw more money at it. That wouldn't work with my corporation. I needed help. I kept being told that computers were the answer. My introduction to them years before was at Jim Bundy's(WD4FZF) in Goldsboro. He'd just gotten that first Radio Shack computer. The very simple programs had to be written in basic and if it was exactly right, you could execute a very, very simple program. I knew right away I wasn't interested. Other than that all I really knew was listening to my two brothers talking gibberish about them at every get-to-gether.

There have been many get-to-gether and parties over the years with me doing several "Pig Pickins", Eastern Carolina Style for Larry in Florida. Boy, that was an interesting bunch of trips. He'd asked me if I would come down a help him with a "Pig Pickin". Sounded like fun to me. Over the ensuing months, it became apparent that it wasn't going to be easy. The pig was a major problem. Seemed there wasn't an outlet for whole pigs in Florida. They were not into the "Pig Picking" thing yet. They didn't even know what real Bar-be-que was. Their idea of Bar-be-que was sliced roast pork with something they called sauce poured over it. About the same thing you get in western Carolina. That tomato based sauce just don't get it. It may be Bar-be-que to them but It sure as hell ain't Down East. He'd finally located one and we were on our way. He'd prepared a cooker according to my instructions and it would work out fine. In fact all his preparations including the two kegs of beer were great. The pig? Now folks that was something else. I'd taken Lester Wood and Billy Sykes with me on the trip. Lester could keep you awake and Billy was a better cook than me. They were also good riding partners. Lester would just keep popping the tops and making trips to the "Porta Potty" in the back. Billy would talk and doze. One thing they were both used to was no stopping. One stop for gas and breakfast was it. that would always be just south of Jacksonville at a Denny's, the gas station was beside it. 10 and ½ hours would do it easily. Once you were on the I-95 super slab, you'd grab a front door and hold on for dear life. The eighteen wheelers would fly you there.

They'd gotten up early, before light on Saturday morning and gone with Larry to pick up the pig while I started the fire and made the pit ready. When they returned, you could tell something was wrong.

"Bobby, you better come out here and look at this."

I was thinking. Oh Hell, what now? What now was a whole hog that had been skinned. YEAH, SKINNED!!!I couldn't believe it. I'd never seen one skinned. Billy said there won't no way to cook and turn it over. Poor Larry's nerves were shot. It was a little after 5 AM. I walked back to the cooker. Stood there for a moment, then walking over to the Kegs, I gulped down three 12 oz. Cups. Walking back to the car, Larry was pleading, he had 100 guests arriving that afternoon. I smiled at him, looked over at Lester and Billy.

"Lets put him on boys."

I'd already fired the pit and it was waiting, we laid him on the rods, covered him with tin foil and I had another 2 cups and set back for a long day. We consumed volumes of beer throughout the day. As the guests began to arrive, we had too. When it was time to turn him over, the moment we were all dreading passed without incident. Knowing the pig would probably fall all to pieces, we used canoe paddles and got the job done. Once it was turned, all looked normal. Of course as per tradition, the tenderloins were gobbled up with copious amounts of my special sauce, more beer, and the final hour began. A good time was had by all and we pulled out at 10 PM for our return trip home. Del had said there won't no damn way she'd ever make that quick turn-around trip again. We'd done it the year before just visiting .

The next year, Larry had made real sure the pig would have it's skin in place. It did, but…. He'd found a farmer that trapped wild pigs, penned and fed them out for six months, then slaughtered them. That was the fattest hog I've ever seen. It weighed about 90 pounds when we put it on and we ended up with less than 20 pounds of usable meat to feed over a hundred people. Needless to say, just like the year before, I consumed many, many cups of brew. I'd also promised myself that this wouldn't happen again. The next year and the years thereafter, I transported the pig from North Carolina. Lester Greene, remember him from the Tower? Built a stainless steel liner for me and I constructed a Cedar box for the liner. I 'd pick up the pig from Teachey's Super Market in Deep Run, pack it in ice, and pull out for Florida. I no longer had an excuse to consume huge volumes of beer, but I never let that bother me. What little I knew about cooking a pig came from back when Jim Grady would cook them under the old barn shelter that I turned into a shop. He'd dig a hole, cover it with "Hog Wire" , fire the pit with hickory coals, cover it all up with pieces of "V" crimp tin, sit back and sip on a jug of "White Lightening".

Eventually the pig would be cooked and he'd be "Stewed." Hey, it worked for him and far as I can tell, I works for me.

For the past several years, Larry's tried to cook his own. He'd asked me to send information about cooking times. This is what I sent him:

INSTRUCTIONS
THE COOKER WILL HAVE TO BE FIRED EVERY 30 TO 45 MINUTES. IF YOU CHOOSE TO USE A BOR-ROWED GAS FIRED ONE, OBVIOUSLY ALL THAT NEEDS TO BE DONE IS KEEP THE TEMPERATURE CHECKED AND DON'T GET BEHIND ON THE BEER.

1- HAVE A BEER.
2- GET PIG WITH SKIN INTACT. HEAD ON FOR BEST PRESENTATION. BLOWS THE GALS MINDS. LITTLE KIDS LOVE IT AND ON A DARE, DRUNKS EAT THE TONGUE, BRAINS AND ANYTHING ELSE HANGING AROUND THAT AREA. THE FEET ARE UP TO YOU. THERE ARE PEOPLE THAT LIKE TO CHEW AND GNAW ON THEM WHILE DRINKING BEER. WHEN I'M THAT DRUNK, FEET AIN'T WHAT I WANTA GNAW ON.

3- HAVE A BEER.

4- COVER THE COOKING AREA WITH TIN FOIL, HEAVY DUTY IS BEST.

5- HAVE A BEER

6- ADD CHARCOAL TO WOOD COALS, THEN SCATTER THEM AROUND THE PIT TO PREHEAT IT.

7- HAVE A BEER.

8- PUT PIG ON, SKIN SIDE UP. NOTE: WE ASSUME PIG AT 50 DEGREES F.

9- THAT'S HARD WORK, HAVE 2 BEERS. OH, COVER THE PIG UP WITH SOMETHING. TIN FOIL, "V" CRIMP TIN, WHATEVER.

10- 2 HOURS LATER, OVEN CAVITY AT 275-300 DEGREES F. PIG BEGINNING TO SLOWLY DRIP. IT IT'S DRIPPING FAST, THROW YOUR THERMOMETER AWAY, IT'S BROKE. GO BACK TO THE OLD METHOD. IF USING TIN, LAY YOUR HAND PALM DOWN ON THE TIN AND COUNT TO THREE. IT SHOULD BE READY TO COME OFF. IF YOU CAN'T HOLD IT TO THREE, PIT'S TOO HOT. IF YOU JUST KEEP COUNTING, TOO COLD. PIG'S READY TO TURN OVER WHEN THE THICKEST PART OF THE HAM IS WARM TO THE TOUCH. I DIDN'T SAY HOT, WARM.

11- HAVE A BEER.

12- 4 HOURS INTO CYCLE. OVEN CAVITY AT 275-300 DEGREES F. MEAT THERMOMETER AIN'T MOVING YET. NOT NECESSARY TO USE IT ANYWAY. JUST HELPS KNOWING WHEN ITS DONE.

13- AT THIS POINT, COOK SHOULD BE NOTICEABLY HAPPY. IF NOT, MORE BEER, LEAST ONE ANYWAY TO BE SURE.

14- 6 HOURS INTO COOKING CYCLE. OVEN CAVITY AT 275-300 DEGREES F. MEAT THERMOMETER IN THICKEST PART OF HAM OR SHOULDER AT 130 F. AND RISING.

15- MORE BEER REQUIRED.

16- 8 HOURS INTO COOKING CYCLE. FUN TIME! TURN THE PIG OVER. CAREFUL! DON'T RUIN IT NOW. AT TIME OF TURNING, MEAT THERMOMETER SHOULD READ 160 DEGREES F. ITS VERY IMPORTANT TO RE-MOVE THE TENDERLOINS AND SAMPLE THE MEAT TO BE SURE IT'S COOKED TO PERFECTION AND THAT THE SAUCE IS JUST RIGHT. NOBODY IS SUPPOSED TO TASTE IT THAT HADN'T BEEN THERE SINCE IF WAS PUT ON. EXCEPTION: THAT GOOD LOOKING GAL OVER THERE IN THE WHITE SHORT/SHORTS OR ANY REASONABLE FACSIMILE. IMPORTANT, REMEMBER THAT THE GOOD LOOKING GAL AT TURNING TIME MIGHT BE A DOG IN THE MORNING. OK? NOW SAUCE THE PIG DOWN REAL GOOD AND COVER IT BACK UP OR YOU WON'T HAVE ANYTHING TO FEED THE MASSES.

17- HAVE ANOTHER BEER.

18- IF BROWNING THE SKIN IS DESIRED, KICK THE TEMPERATURE OF THE OVEN CAVITY UP TO 350 DE-GREES F. CAREFUL, BURNING THE SKIN NOW WILL RUIN THE WHOLE THING.

19- BEER TIME! IF ALL WENT WELL, THE PIG IS READY, IF NOT, WHAT THE HELL! IF YOU'VE FOL-LOWED MY INSTRUCTIONS CORRECTLY, THE PIG IS COOKED AND THE COOK IS "STEWED".

20- NEXT DAY, ASK SOMEBODY HOW IT TURNED OUT.

My special sauce has been forwarded to him each year. What can I say, it's good stuff.

Talking to Larry about computers was a waste. I didn't have the foggiest idea what he was talking about. Hell, all I wanted to do was get some help with my books. I did have the occasion to sit in on one of his classes a few years ago. I certainly was impressed with his teaching methods. Although I didn't have a clue about what he was teaching, the class certainly seemed to.

Ron, on the other hand, was a little easier to communicate with. He'd come down on my level and listen. He also had a computer he wanted to trade in on something bigger. He felt what he had would do just fine for what I wanted. I drove up to Wendell and spent most of a Saturday with him. It all looks so very simple with him at the "Wheel". It had a couple of "DOS" programs including First Choice. It also had a bunch of "stuff" he'd put in there that only he could understand. (He would erase most of its memory before bringing it to me.) I was sure it was just what I needed. A deal was struck and he was to make delivery the following Saturday.

He sat everything up including the printer. The computer was an IBM running at 8 megs. and the printer was a Proprinter. After a couple of hours of me writing down lots of instructions, the money changed hands and he departed. I turned it off almost immediately. Pat had supper ready and so was I. Now friends, what followed, ain't pretty. After supper, I walked back into my office, the converted dining room, sat down and hit the big switch. She came up and went into DOS shell. It hadn't done that before. after hitting every key on it several times and cussing it for all I was worth, I turned it off. Five minutes later, same thing..........

"Ron, this damn thing won't do nothing!"

He could certainly tell I was frustrated. Probably just laid the phone down while I blew. He walked me through the commands and she purred like a kitten. Thanking him, I hung the phone up and POW! Same crap again. All Pat saw for the next few months was the back of my head. The verbal abuse was unreal. It helped me but did little for her or the computer. I finally purchased a book with DOS commands and enrolled at Lenoir Community College for the "Introduction to Computers" class. It didn't take long to realize that I was in the wrong class. I could have cared less about the history of computers. Hell, I just wanted to use the damn thing. Writing basic language programs was crap as far as I was concerned. Besides, I was so close to fifty and friend when you get there, your memory acts just like the RAM in the computer. Turn that sucker off and its gone! Same thing with me. It took me a full week just to remember how to turn the damn thing on. As time went by, redundancy kicked in and I could actually use it. Of course, it was running so slow, you could turn it on and go take a bath waiting for it to come up. Reminded me of something else. Of course you didn't realize how slow it was until you got the next one. Then you knew! I didn't really have the programs I needed for bookkeeping . The hard drive was much too small for any of the new programs coming out so I purchased my first new computer, a clone, 6 months later. It was running at 33 megs. and had 4 megs of Ram. Its hard drive was up to 250 megs.

That was a bunch back then and had the new innovative CD ROM drive. Along with the package was the updated Windows 3.0, a mouse, and several software packages including Quicken . That's been my saving grace over the past 8-9 years. I upgrade very often and really put a lot of trust in the program. Reconciling is easy and not dreaded anymore. That program along with "My Product Invoices" and "Home CAD" allows me to offer a complete package to my customers. Using a program called "AutoQuotes", doing quotations and purchase orders is a snap. Updated monthly, it's perfect for my little "one horse" operation. I've upgraded computers several times trying the Dell pentium 90, (by far, the best so far)Hewlett Packard Vectra and Compaq Presario. When I ordered the Dell, it arrived on a weekend while Pat was at the beach. When she returned, I told her that Dell, all she heard was Del (my ex.) had come to visit and was still there. Pat tore into the house and took it apart. You never heard such goings on in your life.

"All right, where is she?"

"She who?"

"Don't give me that crap, Where is she?"

Laughing, I walked with her into my office space and pointed to the new computer. She took one look at the label and threatened to kill me.

With the advent of Windows 95 and now 98, the requirements for storage are unbelievable. My hard-drive now has 8.5 GIGS and its running at 300 megs with 128 megs of Ram. The ROM is 40X and its all obsolete. Every six months, the computers change. I'm totally dependent on them now utilizing software programs to design layouts, invoice customers and do quotations. The quotation program alone, AutoQuotes, eats up almost a half GIG of space and grows with each monthly update (it also includes spec. sheets). When's the last time you completely backed up your hard drive. What do you mean, never? When I first started, it all fitted on a "B" drive 5" Floppy, then one 3 ½" A drive floppy with .75 megs. of storage, then the 1.44 meg. floppys. Now, I use the Iomega Zip drive with 100 megs. on each disk and with compression, that triples it's capacity and it still take 6 of those and 1 ½ hours to complete. Unbelievable!

Looking back over my computer experiences, I still find it very difficult to understand what my apprehension was when it came to computers. I'd been on the cutting edge with so many other technologies in the past. Just talking to different people that haven't gotten on board, leaves me more confused. The excuses are abundant. Some sound so reasonable and logical, they're almost believable. I was with Janet Farrar the other day. She's the Child Nutrition Director for Warren County Schools. Kizzy, her secretary was just outside her office, backing up the files in her computer so they could be transferred into the new one. It had the iomega Zip drive built in. No more messing with a stack of 1.44 disks. Somewhere in our conversation, Janet made mention of the fact she wasn't computer literate yet. Oh yes, she had a computer, down stairs, but not in her office. Her's was the last office that didn't have one on the desk. She played solitary on it, but that was it. I'm sure Cousin Lucy used it more that she. Cousin Lucy? You'll enjoy this. The board of education presently occupies a beautiful old home. Very spacious and grand, it was built years earlier by a gentleman wanted a place to spend the summers. Bringing the family down, they would wile away the summers in the cool breezes under the massive tree canopies and just enjoy the rolling country side. If I recall correctly, Cousin Lucy was the unmarried sister of the owner and died in the house. Story goes that she's been seen many, many times over the years in the many different rooms and levels of the house. Jim Sweeney, the Vulcan Hart representative and I were given the grand tour when we called on Janet for the first time there. She'd been the Director in Martin County before taking this position and we called on her there. One of the ladies we were introduced to was the daughter of the Contractor that built the house. Listening to her recounting stories of its construction was absolutely fascinating. Our parting question to Janet before leaving was how often she worked late in her office alone.

"Never! Bob Holt, you'll never catch me in here alone!"

That seemed to be the sentiment of everyone there. Though they were laughing, we could all feel Cousin Lucy standing there with us. Janet says she'll be on line soon. There's so many subjects she'd interested including family history and I promise you there's something about each subject on the world wide web. If I have nothing better to do. I'll spend hours looking at real estate around the world. It's unbelievable how many properties absolutely fill you every dream. Now if I can just figure out how to afford it.

Communications? Oh yes. Totally automated with the Brother MFC 1950 "All in One" plain paper fax, printer, copier, scanner, fax modem and message center with digital answering.

Sure its a plain paper fax machine. What do you take me for? Anyone that's ever been the proud recipient of one of Scott Murhpy's 20 page Colorpoint fax quotations delivered on the old thermal paper machines, prayed for the new one. I've walked into my office, seems like hundreds of times, just to be presented with a roll of thermal paper covering half the room. After ten minutes of cutting the individual pages, dropping them twice, re-sorting them, stapling them and trying to get that curled up mess to lay flat, I was ready to mortgage my home to get one of those new fangled plain paper machines. What happened after I got it? Exactly, outdated the very next day. Now the computer does all that for you. Sending, receiving and unless you need a paper trail, it all stays inside the computer. Bring them on Scott, I'm ready for you now.

Of course I'm online, ain't everybody. I've been on AOL for several years. (BobLHolt@AOL.com) I began with Prodigy, then jumped to AOL staying until it became so log-jammed, the only time you could get past the busy signal was 3 AM. OK, OK, yes I did get up in the seventies and talk "skip" at three. That was different. If you were lucky enough to finally get on, the first attempt at retrieving your mail was met with. "Try again later, we're unable to retrieve your mail at this time." You've just spent 30 minutes just getting online just to be told to try again later. The speed of the modem was something akin to a turtle that had just been told that when he reached the other side of the road, he'd die, or like the guy in front of you on the company pick-up running 30 miles an hour. Looking at your watch, you realize its 4:30 PM. The SOB is going to make sure he won't get back to the plant until quitting time at five. That's pretty close to the speed of my first modem. I'd get so frustrated, I'd stomp out of the room, eat a snack, drink a beer, sometimes two, walk to the mailbox, anything to get away from that one eyed "Slow Boat to China." What really jerked your chain, it was by the minute. Sure it was, remember? None of that one fee, no time limit then and on top of that, there was no local number in Kinston. It was all long distance. Arriving in Winterville, three years ago, I tried a local server. In the beginning, it was much better but almost immediately I had problems. The system didn't seem to recognize me at all. It was though everything was on Ram and when you turned that sucker off, amnesia set in. The very next time I tried to go on line. Who the hell are you? My server didn't have a clue. Back to the drawing board, dump all the cuss words out on the floor. I'd need all of them. Try reinstalling the program using the supplied disk. Part of the time, that would work, even if it did, there'd go another hour of your time and if that didn't do the job, what then? What then was attempting to delete the program and starting over. With no undelete built into the program, resorting to a program such as Norton would maybe or maybe not get rid of all those little goodies, especially the ones ending in .dll hiding in Windows/System and some other yet discovered little nook or cranny. Of course if the TCP/IP's and other goodies hidden in the network connection programs only accessible through the Control Panel icon weren't deleted, adjusted or reinstalled correctly. Nothing would work. It you were trying to start over from square one. Delete the whole damn thing. There's certainly a better way. Of course, I don't have a clue what it is and take a pretty dim view of having to pay some geek at hundred bucks an hour to get it done. A call to the server hooked me up with someone that was obviously from the beginning, very irritated at being bothered. He probably was in the midst of some diabolical scheme to screw the untutored public or on one of those wed sites that Momma would turn over in her grave it she knew what he was doing. Here I am trying to explain my problem to this computer brained bastard and he acted as if I belonged in a kindergarten class. Very quickly I apologized for bothering him muttering under my breath something to the effect that he was lower than whale droppings and that was in the bottom of the ocean. After two or three more hours and more cussing, ranting and raising hell, I finally got back online. Now what was I looking for? I didn't have a clue. Two hours late for my appointment. Madder than the poor guy that had been told for the past year his wife couldn't have sex because of something he couldn't pronounce and finding the doctor who'd told him that crap, in bed with his wife, banging each other's eyeballs out. There ain't enough Rogaine and Propecia in the world to keep hair on my head worrying about my computer and internet woes. I could take a bath in Rogaine and it wouldn't help. Sure, I'd have long curly locks everywhere but where I wanted them.

Just at that low point, what does the mailman deliver to your door? We've missed you. Come on back to AOL now. Its easy, just insert this disk in your drive and follow the easy directions. Within minutes, I was on line with my old e-mail address and loving it.

"Hello local SOB server. I'm terminating my contract with you."

"Why Mr. Holt?"

"Just want to. I'm not happy here."

"You'll have to send us a letter or e-mail us."

"Fine, goodbye."

It was an absolute pleasure e-mailing them from AOL. But, of course, you guessed it. AOL is beginning to log jam again.

Naturally the changes in addresses created havoc with my friends online. Going from BobHolt to BobLHolt was confusing to say the least. Some poor soul out in the Midwest was inundated with e-mail that apparently didn't belong to him, at first he tried to explain, soon he gave it up. As we all know, that's what the delete button is for.

Now let me tell you about the delete button. Please bow and salute, you're in the presence of a master deleter. That one word has kept me in more trouble than all the other things I've ever done combined. From the beginning, it was trouble, big trouble. In the dos programs, delete meant just that. I'd beat the keyboard almost to a pulp trying to type in the correct dos command and when it would finally do it, I'd cry. God, I didn't need to do that. After spending an hour trying to get your foot outta you're butt. You'd promise yourself never, ever to do that again. Ever done that? How long did it last? About the same here. I've lost business records, complete databases, games, you name it, I've lost it. Type in the correct command, Are You Sure? Yes/No. Hell yes I'm sure. Damnit all, I've done it again. I continue doing it now, although most of the time, I can recover. Learning to utilize the backup systems and dumping unwanted goodies into the Recycle bin gives me the opportunity to recant. I did dump my hard drive once. I'd purchased a new computer and wanted to give the old one to Pat's granddaughter. Letting Pat use the one I was replacing. You're right, one thing I have plenty of, is computers. What are you suppose to do with the old ones, nobody except a church will give you anything for it. Teri is almost sixteen and really needs and computer. Its almost impossible now to do what's expected of a student in school without one. Over the five years I'd had "Miss Dell". I'd made lots of mistakes removing programs and using the big DELETE button. Always going where no one's been before, I could trash a program in a heartbeat. Being in the Windows files was something akin to a bull in a china shop, same results. I'd delete a file that didn't look right, bang! Next time the computer would come, first thing you get was messages telling you Windows was looking for some file and couldn't find it. I'd close that banner and the next one would appear. I tried re-installing Windows, upgrading Windows, anything to get rid of those unwanted prompts. Nothing had worked. I knew one thing would though and since I was giving it to Teri, I didn't want her confused with all those weird prompts. Being very sure that's what I wanted to do, I proceeded. At first it absolutely refused, giving me thousands of opportunities to back down. Not me! By God, I was going to gut this baby, one way or the other. Little by little it's defenses began to break down. I was having to chop this tree down, one limb at the time. Finally closing windows, I began to delete from the dos side. Being very close to senility, stuff I don't use almost daily, hides from me or completely vanishes. Trying to remember dos commands from seven or eight years ago was humbling to say the least. I'm being nice now. after most of the morning, my patience was completely gone, if I ever really had any, and my expletives were gushing forth by the bushels. Being totally comfortable in that environment, I began to move forward. Moving back and forth between C:\DOS AND C:\, the root directory, stuff was beginning to disappear. Finally getting rid of the Windows directory completely, my command to format "C" was finally accepted. After reading that screen one last time; Are You Sure? Yes/No.

"You bet your ass, I'm sure!"

I banged out Yes and hit enter. Within moments that drive was as clean as a spanked baby's behind. I couldn't believe it. I'd finally gotten rid of everything. Oh yes, I do mean everything. Shutting her down and then bringing her back up got you a blinking curser. That's all, no c:, no nothing. I promise you my joy would be short lived.

First I installed Dos; 6.2, followed by Sound Blaster 16 and then adaptec EZ-SCSI. I was on a roll. Anybody could do this. What was the problem? My roll abruptly ended. All my tires blewout. Miss Dell wouldn't recognize the ROM drive. No way was there a "D" drive in this computer. Hell, I'd take care of that. Popping the emergency Windows startup disk, I brought her up again. I'm smart, what can I tell you........This is an update version of Windows 95, we cannot detect a previous version. What the hell is this? Update my do-do hole! Sure enough, splashed across the front of the disk. Windows 95, update version. Digging through everything I owned couldn't produce any previous Windows version. Everything I had was an update. Even my Windows 98 was an update. Back to square one, what now?

"Ron, hower you doing?"

"Busier than a one legged man climbing up a ladder. School along with church and my job about to get me. What's up?"

He knew something must be. All we ever did was e-mail anymore.

"Developed a little computer problem and was hoping you'd be able to help me."

I told him the story and he assured me he had right disks. I'd offered to give him a laptop I never used and it would be a good time to pick it up. Saturday was set, til then, there was nothing I could do. Teri and Faye had planned to come that weekend. I'd asked Pat to set it back one week. Ron arrived and with minutes set my mind to ease. Nothing to it if you've got the right stuff. We had a chance to visit a bit before he left. That's a rarity for us. Guess it's the same with most folks anymore. After church on Sunday, I finished installing the programs I thought Teri would use.

I finished up the surprise I'd been working on since Christmas for Faye. We were at Pat's Mom's for Christmas lunch and afterwards while doing the dishes, Faye noticed the trash container I'd crafted for the Kentucky Fried Queen, (I've mentioned Pat's mom, Lucille before. She's petite, very neat, glasses and very scheduled. When I met her and Slim, Pat's step father, about 10 years ago, (They live in Danville, VA.) Lucille was a closet smoker and would eat just about anything set before her. She had something like Psoriasis on her thumb and had practically stopped cooking much to Slim's chagrin. Didn't take a lot to make him happy, buttermilk and biscuits would do it everytime. He waits on her hand and foot, and she sure as hell lets him. Lucille would on occasion prepare for us but mostly it was a trip to Mary's Diner that got us fed. Six or seven years ago, she had bypass surgery and was told by the Doctor's that smoking and anything that tasted good was history. The smoking stopped but,

"I really shouldn't have this. Maybe just a little taste, chomp, chomp, chomp."

Picking up any and everything including Bar-be-que, country ham, it made no difference. We all learned to ignore her excuses. A few years ago, someone suggested picking up a chicken package from Kentucky Fried. Slim and I ran the errand and returned with more than enough for our group. Lucille took one look at those luscious pieces of fried chicken and went on it like a hog on slops. Our visits usually lasted 3 to 4 hours and then it was time for the 3 hour trip back home. About an hour into the trip, I told Pat that we should call and tell Lucille we'd been visiting some friends and would be stopping by for the chicken leftovers before we left Danville. I could see her standing there motioned to Slim go rush out and replace what she'd eaten the moments we left. I'd called her the Kentucky Fried Queen during the meal and it stuck. I was recording bits and pieces of the festivities and cleaning up was part of it. Faye asked if I'd make one for her and I'd promised to try. Faye's an absolute bird freak with owl's being on the top of the list. After putting the pieces together and applying two coats of white paint, I'd brought it into my office to decorate. The removable top was shaped like a gabled house roof, complete with a chimney with round knob on top. The sides were decorated with different kinds of birds, trees and flowers. There were a couple of red birds, a blue bird, dove and a couple more. Dogwood flowers along with apple blossoms rounded it out. An owl was the highlight on the back panel along with a little mouse peeking up at him from the tall grass.

They came down the following weekend which happened to be Easter. Teri was on the computer immediately. I'd set it up in the upstairs bedroom that Pat's computer was in. Sunday morning I slipped Faye's present along with an Easter Basket for Pat into the kitchen. Faye cried tears of joy. She was overwhelmed. I'll remember that for quite a while. I sent word to Teri's Pa-Pa that I'd furnished the computer, the least he could do would be furnish the printer. Ain't happened yet. I don't understand some people and when it comes to children, my not having any of my own completely leaves me out in the cold. I outta know, I've been told that enough times over the past ten years.

Back to the internet, that's certainly the communications of the future. Kinda interesting though, can't call "Breaker, Breaker" anymore. Now it's YOU'VE GOT MAIL! Just like in the old days with some of the breakers. You didn't want anything to do with some of them and you sure as hell don't want some of that unsolicited E-mail. Just as before, you didn't have to acknowledge the breaker and you darn sure don't have to read the unwanted mail. I don't care where you go or what you do, there will always be a "Cosmo" around.

Of course if you're on AOL, the buddy system alerts you when one of your friends or family are on line and you can carry on a live QSO via the keyboard. No, it sho nuff ain't like talking in that microphone and CB slang ain't near as much fun trying to type it as say. In fact, just like right now, I find it almost impossible to put down how it sounds in person. God, seems everything I do now is computer generated. If the Y2K bug or Sunspot cycle 23 does reek havoc. Guess I'll just have to go on vacation for awhile. Even though transportation might be so screwed up that it's unusable. The car's still there. Guess the gas stations won't be operating though. And if they are, they probably won't be able to take your credit card, (oh, you got green money in your pocket? Enough to last you how long? I sure don't, maybe enough for a six pak or two. Sure wouldn't want to have to live a week off of it.) because of the "Solar Disturbances". Hell, probably have to stay home and use the radio. Yeah, Yeah, the Power Company didn't prepare for 2000 and Y2K shut them down. Guess I'll just have to walk out the front door and holler at my neighbor. He's probably outside too. Too hot in the house without air-conditioning. Maybe I should install a "Wind Powered Generator." That way I could still operate some of my communications equipment. Trouble with that, if you didn't do the same thing, how could I communicate with you. Guess we could "Eyeball" each other. That won't work either, most of us don't live close enough. It would take all day to visit someone 10 miles away. Guess that's out too. Sure I can walk 10 miles, But not today!

Regardless of which way I go. My start was in CB and my special memories will always be there. Many, many times when I least expect it. there will be a.........

"Breaker, Breaker, Cousin."

It might be Crackerjack, Monkey Wrench, Night Hawk, or Insurance Man, or maybe you.

"Go ahead breaker, Cousin gotcha."

As Bob Hope said many times.

"Thanks for the Memories."

Some of the many contacts in 1974, 1975, 1976, and 1977

ALLIS CHAMLER	KENANSVILLE, NC
A FARMALL	MOUNT OLIVE, NC
AQUA VELVA	MIDDLESEX, NC
BOBCAT	JACKSONVILLE, NC
BOOT HILL	JACKSONVILLE, NC
BRICK HAMMER	JACKSONVILLE, NC
BLACK HAWK	GOLDSBORO, NC
POWER WAGON	GOLDSBORO, NC
BRONCO BUSTER	ROSE HILL, NC
BLUE JAY	CYPRESS CREEK, NC
BILL BAILEY	TURKEY, NC
GOBLER	TURKEY, NC
NECK TIE	TURKEY, NC
BLUE DEVIL	PINK HILL, NC
BLUE DRAGON	DEEP RUN, NC
BUTCHER MAN	SMITHFIELD, NC
BLUE BIRD	ROSE HILL, NC
BANKER BOY	PINK HILL, NC
BULL DOZER	KINSTON, NC
BANJO MAN	
BOMBSHELL	ROSE HILL, NC
BOILER MAN	RICHLANDS, NC
HARVEY #1	KINSTON, NC
HARRY "O"	KINSTON, NC
21 W 263, SANDY	HUDSON, ILL.
CRACKERJACK	ALBERTSON, NC
CRICKET MAN	BEULAVILLE, NC
CHARLIE HORSE	PINE LEVEL, NC
COTTON TOP	WALLACE, NC
COUNTRY GIRL	KENANSVILLE, NC
CHIPMONK	ALBERTSON, NC
CAROLINA MAX	KINSTON, NC
COSMO	KINSTON, NC
CRAWDAD	BEULAVILLE, NC
CATFISH	CHINQUAPIN, NC
COTTON	ALBERTSON, NC
COMPOST BABE	GOLDSBORO, NC
CHUBBY	KINSTON, NC
CHICKEN MAN	ROSE HILL, NC

CHARLIE BROWN	KINSTON, NC
DOLPHIN	GOLDSBORO, NC
DODGE MAN	SNOW HILL, NC
411	GOLDSBORO, NC
FIFTH WHEEL MOBILE	MT. OLIVE, NC
FLYROD	GREENVILLE, NC
FOUNTAINTOWN BOY	FOUNTAINTOWN, NC
GRASSHOPPER	ALBERTSON, NC
GOSHEN MAN	KENANSVILLE, NC
GOSHENEER	KENANSVILLE, NC
GOSHEN MOBILE	KENANSVILLE, NC
GOVENOR	BURGAW, NC
GREASE MONKEY	
GARLAND MOBILE	GARLAND, NC
GREEN SIX	WOODINGTON, NC
GRAY DOG	WARSAW, NC
GREEN APPLE	ALBERTSON, NC
GO GETTER	NEW BERN
GIRL WATCHER	KINSTON, NC
GREEN HORNET	HARRELLS CROSS ROADS
GAS MAN	WHITEVILLE, NC
GOOSENECK	WALLACE, NC
HOG MAN	WARSAW, NC
HORNET MAN	KENANSVILLE, NC
HARRY "Q"	KINSTON, NC
HAWK	KENANSVILLE, NC
HAMMER HEAD	KINSTON, NC
INSURANCE MAN	SANDY BOTTOM, NC
JUNK MAN	WALLACE, NC
LITTLE ABNER	PENDER COUNTY, NC
LONE RANGER	DEEP RUN, NC
LITTLE CRICKET	GREENVILLE, NC
LITTLE PICKLE	MT. OLIVE, NC
LELAND MOBILE	LELAND, NC
LITE FOOT	
LITTLE BEAVER	WALLACE, NC
LITTLE BEAVER SQUAW	WALLACE, NC
LAZY MAN	TEACHEY, NC
LOUD MOUTH	TEACHEY, NC
MOPAR	RICHLANDS, NC
MISS KITTY	ALBERTSON, NC
MONKEY WRENCH	DEEP RUN, NC

GRANDMA	DEEP RUN, NC
MUSTANG TWO	BEULAVILLE, NC
MISS KITTY	KINSTON, NC
MISS KITTY	GOLDSBORO, NC
NOMAD	JACKSONVILLE, NC
MIGHTY MOBILE	BURMUDA
OMEGA MAN	JACKSONVILLE, NC
ORANGE PEEL	ROSE HILL, NC
PETER GUN BASE	RICHLANDS, NC
PIPE MAN	BEULAVILLE, NC
PIPE LADY	BEULAVILLE, NC
PHAROAH	BEULAVILLE, NC
PINK HILL 1	PINK HILL, NC
POPEYE	WALLACE, NC
PAINT MAN	BURGAW, NC
RED MAN	PINK HILL, NC
RED BARON	CLAYTON, NC
RATTLESNAKE	KENANSVILLE, NC
ROAD HOG	WALLACE, NC
ROSE HILL MAN	ROSE HILL, NC
RED HILL BABE	SCOTT'S STORE
ROUND MAN	FAYETTEVILLE, NC
RED BARON	KINSTON, NC
RAG MAN	KINSTON, NC
RED TOYOTA	
SONG BIRD	WARSAW, NC
SKIPPER	PINK HILL, NC
SILVER DOLLAR	JACKSONVILLE, NC
SCARE CROW	BEULAVILLE, NC
SQUIRREL	TEACHEY, NC
SUPER "B"	CHINQUAPIN, NC
SHEEP DOG	BEULAVILLE, NC
STORE MAN	BEULAVILLE, NC
STRAW BABY	BEULAVILLE, NC
SUGAR BEAR	GRIFTON, NC
SNEAKY SNAKE	JACKSONVILLE, NC
SLIM	KINSTON, NC
SUPERSPORT	BEULAVILLE, NC
SPOT	PINK HILL, NC
SUITCASE	BLADENBORO, NC
THUNDERBIRD	KINSTON, NC
TRIPLE NICKEL	GREENVILLE, NC

TREE DOG	WARSAW, NC
TURKEY	ALBERTSON, NC
TINY	RICHLANDS, NC
TERMITE	CABIN, NC
THUNDER	TEACHEY, NC
TOMCAT	GOLDSBORO, NC
TENNESSEE DRIFTER	JACKSONVILLE, NC
UNIT ONE	KINSTON, NC
VARONA BASE	VARONA, NC
NIGHT HAWK	DEEP RUN, NC
RED MAN	JONESTOWN, NC
WOODPECKER	DEEP RUN, NC
WRECKER MAN	
WHITE TURKEY	PINK HILL, NC WALLACE, NC
WART HOG	HALLSVILLE, NC
WHIP	WARSAW, NC
WARSAW BASE	PINK HILL, NC
YELLOW DOG	LA GRANGE, NC
DAVY CROCKET	BRUCETON, TN.
LITTLE FELLOW	HALIFAX, NOVA SCOTIA
W.B. 1356	ELWOOD, KANSAS
UNIT 308	ALBANY, GA.
SOUTH GEORGIA MOBILE	ORILLA, ONT. CANADA
CANADIAN SQUEEK	MARAZAIBO CITY, VENEZUELA
ANGEL	LONGVIEW TX.
OUTLAW	SPRING HILL, NOVA SCOTIA
BATMAN	ST. GEORGE, ONT. CANADA
POLAR BEAR	WESTVILLE, NOVA SCOTIA
GLOBEMASTER	MEDELLIN, COLUMBIA
AIRMAIL 1960	SODBURY, ONT. CANADA
HAPPY HERMIT	LOYAL, WISC.
UNIT 308	TROUP, TX.
MUD DAUBER	MYRTLE, MISS.
SLIM	BENNETTSVILLE, SC.
EL DORADO	ST JAMES, MISS.
HIWAY MAN	STELLERTON, NOVA SCOTIA
RED ROOSTER	PITCHFIELD, MASS.
LITTLE ONE	LOVANN, ARK.
THE OLDS	STREATOR, ILL.
351	HAZELHURST, MISS.
SKEETER BEATER	DEARBORN, MICH.
BIG APACHE	BRAXTON, MISS.

PETER RABBIT	ELIZABETHTOWN, NC
251	SARETTA, LA.
DOUBLE M	HUDSON, ILL.
21-W-263, STANLEY	MIAMI, FLA.
UNIT 394, DOUG.	NEW GLASSGLOW, NOVA SCOTIA
TRIPLE 7	CONWAY, MICH.
HF-3188	AMSTERDAM, NY
HFA-2810	FAYETTEVILLE,NC
AM	POINT CLEAR, ALA.
HFLSB	MERIDAN, KANSAS
HFX-8274	KENGSHA, WISC.
MR PEPPER	MONCTON, NEW BRUNSWICK
V1E3, BILL	MONCTON, NEW BRUNSWICK
PEP401, DENNY	MONTEGO BAY, JAMAICA
TIGER	SPRINGFIELD MASS.
WAYNE, LSB	BURLINGTON, IOWA
UNIT 23'	FORT EUSTIS, VA.
ROAD RUNNER	HALIFAX, NOVA SCOTIA
SHY BOY	HALIFAX, NOVA SCOTIA
MARSHALL	WESTVILLE, NOVA SCOTIA
FIREMAN	WARTON, NOVA SCOTIA
PLAYCAT	BEDFORD, NOVA SCOTIA
POOR BOY	HALIFAX, NOVA SCOTIA
HOT RODDER	TANGIER, NOVA SCOTIA
PUDDLE JUMPER	ESMOND, RI
SANDY	COLFAX, ILL.
UNIT 7800	QUINSEY, ILL.
FREIGHT TRAIN	HIALEAH, FLA.
UNIT 42	PARSIPPANY, NJ
3-W-50, PETE	CORUNNA, ONT. CANADA
CLEANING MACHINE	PORT HURON, MICH.
PAT & GAIL	WOONSOCKET, RI
HANK	SPRING HILL, NOVA SCOTIA
RON	HOWELL, MICH.
KRM 5711	LIMOILOV, QUEBEC, CANADA
MIMI	GOLDSBORO, NC
BOOTLEGGER	GRAND TURK ISLAND, W. INDIES
HFX 3502, EBEN	METAIRIE, LA.
X5364	PASADENA, TX.
KING OF THE ROAD	NORRISTOWN, PA.
COALMINER	WHITEHORSE, YUKON TERRITORY
SNOWSHOE	MONROE, LA.

X-CHANGER	KINNELON, NJ
RAWHIDE	NORTHBAY, ONT. CANADA
ORGAN GRINDER	HUTCHINSON, KANSAS
BOOKER	VINTON, LA.
18-W-2759, VINCE	GOLDSBORO, NC
12-W-342, JAKE	KINSTON, NC
KHC-81, DON	KINSTON, NC
KHC-82, GATOR	CLAYTON, NC
KHC-83, LESTER	WARSAW, NC
KHC-84, BUCK	JACKSONVILLE, NC
KHC-85, JIM	JACKSONVILLE, NC
KHC-86, GROUND HOG	
KHC-87, MARVIN	KINSTON, NC
KHC-90, WALTER	KINSTON, NC
KHC-93, WALTER	
HKC-96, RAYMOND	OCEAN ISLE BEACH, NC
NC-1563, ALLEN	LARENBURG, NC
NC-2012, JACK	RALEIGH, NC
NC-462, HERB	
12-W-317, HENRY	
12-W-328, RICHARD	GLENDALE, ARIZ.
UNIT 651	
VHF 3455, JERRY	
9-W-166, SUE	ST. LEWIS, ILL.
HFX-3195, ARCHIE	MAINE
HFB-3107, GEORGE	SAN JUAN, PUERTO RICA
NF-12, WALT	SNEEDS FERRY, NC
WF1, TOM	NEWPORT, NC
NC-308, JOE	MONCTON, NEW BRUNSWICK
HF-354, BILL	MELBOURNE, FLA.
HCF-390, DENNIS	LANNON, IOWA
30-W-828, MONTY	LANNON, IOWA
30-W-618, STEVE	LANNON, IOWA
30-W-895, TONY	PERRY, ILL.
HFB-2922	MUSKETADEEN, IOWA
29-W-2003, PAUL	DEEP RUN, NC
UNIT 303, SNAPPER	MIDWAY, NC
12-W-472, JESSIE	CAPE HATTERAS, NC
12-W-466, SAM	PAUARES, FLA.
VHF-2502, MAYNARD	MELROSE, FLA.
27-W-62, HERB	MELROSE, FLA.
27-W-29, BILL	BUNKIE, LA.

18-W-3466, RAYMOND	SHOE, TEXAS
28-W-1215, OSCAR	WARSAW, NC
DU-37, LYNN	JACKSONVILLE, NC
CR-194, LYNN	ARK.
CA-211, WOODY	KANSAS
RANGER SIX	GOLDSBORO, NC
ENC-6, JOE	GITMO. BAY, CUBA
HFB-1647, BUD	BURLINGTON, IOWA
VHF-301A, JONN	IOWA
FE-15	ST LEWIS, MO.
MO-55, JOHN	PHOENIX, ARIZ.
HFA-920, MARY	LOS ANGELES, CA.
VHF-2389, TERRY	PINK HILL, NC
FROG MAN	PINK HILL, NC
COOKIE	MARANA, ARIZ.
KFA-3519, JOHN	MARANA, ARIZ.
KFA-1315, MARCHETTA 62-W-15, ED	GAMBOA, PANAMA CANAL, GUADALAJARA, MEXICO
HFA-2456, JOSE	ELDON, IOWA
29-W-007,	RALEIGH, NC
12-W-229, JL	RALEIGH, NC
NC-1236, BENNY	
NC-1428, MIKE	
NC-1446, RICHARD	GOLDSBORO, NC
NC-731, JIMMY	OCEANSIDE, CALIF.
HF-278, DICK	CORPUS CHRISTA, TX.
28-W-313, EILANE	TEXAS
28-W-33, JOHN	
46-W-2, JIM	
46-W-65, BOB	
46-W-66, AL	VERMONT
14-W-6, KATHY	PA.
X-7389,	DATONA BEACH, FLA.
HFA-2038, DAVE	DATONA BEACH, FLA
HFA-2037, SONDRA	ONT. CANADA
54-W-21, RALPH	FLA.
27-W-489, MEL	MASS.
6-W-923, MIKE	DETROIT, MICH.
HF-936,	NEW ENGLAND
6-W-137, ART	NEW ENGLAND
6-W-91, DON	NOVA SCOTIA
NC-129, WILLARD	CAPLEN, ONT. CANADA

HFX-5807, ROGER	MICH.
WDX-86, BILL	BOURBONLAND, IND.
BM-107	OK.
JINGLE JANGLES	CONWAY, SC
PLUMBERBOY	CONWAY, SC
RADIATOR BASE	POINT FORTIN, TRINIDAD, W. INDIES
495	PANAMA CANAL ZONE, ALBROOK AFB
62-W-190, JOHN	WALLACE, NC
NC-1232, EVERETT	MICHIGAN
BOOTLEGGER 1803	LA.
TDR-115, CHARLES	FLA.
FLA 1307	
2633, TONY	OK.
ARK 155, LARRY	
OHF 2101, KEITH	NEW ORLEANS, LA.
HFX 8944, CARL	MISSOURI
HF 8748, CHARLES	NEW ORLEANS, LA.
18-W-656, JEAN	HAMSHIRE, TN.
TSB 100, SPARKIE	ONT. CANADA
FENDER BENDER	ROSE CITY, MICH.
GOLDEN SCREW DRIVER	MICH.
RED BIRD	MICH.
POKEY	HARRELLSVILLE, NC
NC-958	WINSTON-SALEM, NC
NC-496, LUTHER	PITTSBORO, NC
NC-693	S. CAROLINA
SC-099	GOLDSBORO, NC
BOOTLEGGER 1723	GOLDSBORO, NC
DONALD DUCK	BOGOTA, COLUMBIA
99 STATION	BOGOTA, COLUMBIA
HK4, WILLIAM	FLORIDA KEYS
NC-332	TULSA OK.
46-W-13, RON	MO.
24 E 170, DON	S. TEXAS
HF 9160, JERRY	CLEVELAND, OHIO
17-W-841, CARL	DANVILLE, VA.
10-W-2, BOB	FORT WAYNE, IND.
19-W-559, MIKE	VA.
1499, LYNN	MIAMI, FLA.
3216, LARRY	VALLEY FORGE, PA.
X 3028, PAUL	VIRGINIA
HF 2339	HAMPTON, VA.

VHF 1131, ED
VHF 2190, BUTCH   IND.
VHF 1532, PETE
VHF 717, CHARLIE   MISSOURI
CHIMNEY SWEEPER   COMPTON, QUEBEC
7013   JACKSONVILLE, FLA.
X 3473, CLYDE   JACKSONVILLE, FLA.
WATER MOBILE   TAMPA, FLA.
X 759   ORLANDO, FLA.
BIG JIM   POINT HARBOR, TRINIDAD, W. INDIES
UNIT 73,   LEWISVILLE, OHIO
UNIT 42   HIALEAH, FLA.
FLC 141   MIAMI, FLA.
GUITAR MAN   S. MIAMI, FLA.
TRIPLE DUCE   MICH.
WINDY   DETROIT, MICH
TOM CAT   SATALITE BEACH, FLA.
20-W-258, HOYT
A 1415, PHILIX   SHREVEPORT, LA.
X 9693, DAN   FLA.
HF 2663, RANDY   CARSON CITY, NEVADA
LADY   BUTTER SPRING, KANSAS
LADY   ALBERTSON, NC
STUMP JUMPER   MISSOURI
FREIGHT TRAIN   QUINCEY, OHIO
SWEET LADY   ILL.
BUCKET MOUTH   ILL.
UNCLE FUDD   COLFAX, ILL.
21-W-301   ILL.
DIAMOND JIM   WAYNESVILLE, MISSOURI
STRAWBERRY CONTROL   OAKLAHOMA CITY, OK.
516   OK.
HFA 741, SONNY   HERB, TX.
CRYSTAL   TX.
JAN 1   SARASODA, FLA.
HF 2562, WES
UNIT 23   BURLINGTON, IOWA
SALTY DOG   ILL.
SALTY DOG   KINSTON, NC
SENATOR   MINN.
44   IOWA
6-W-168, WAYNE   SPRINGFIELD, MASS

32-W-194, TOM   MINN.
26-W-13, LEE   DETROIT, MICH.
26-W-213   DETROIT, MICH
X 179, JOHN   OHIO
X 4419   OHIO
ZIZZY   RUSHFORD, MINN
32-W-43, DON
25-W-26, WAYNE   MINN.
X 6968, MERLIN
29-W-211
A-630, JOHN
MC 927, GARY
3347   ILL.
21-W-448, SAM   ILL.
WVE 707, WALT   MISSOURI
21-W-516, CHARLES
HF 1479, DAVE
21-W-263, STANLEY
3-W-226
HFA-3190, MILL
TIGER   MONTEGO BAY, JAMAICIA
KCX 591, JESS   WILMINGTON, NC
NA 269, DENNY   NEW BRUNSWICK
A-829   MICH
3-W-124
HF 2205, JERRY   TOLEDO, OHIO
A 2942
HFA 829, ERNIE   MICH
HFA 2941, KEITH   MICH
HFX 8154, AL   MICH.
HF 7665, CHARLIE   MICH.
JJ 25, JACK   MICH
26-W-407   MICH.
51-W-20   NOVA SCOTIA
HF 6568, JOHN   MICH.
32-W-43   MINN.
NC 1072, LUKE
HFA 1532, HARVEY   WALSTONBURG, NC
HFX 691, BILLY   LARGO, FLA.
HF 9444, HANK   LARGO, FLA.
HF 9448,   LARGO, FLA.
HF 2148, RICHARD   LA.

TXC 526, HERB	MARYLAND
488, TED	ALBERTA, CANADA
VHF 3, JOHN	CHICAGO, ILL.
VHF 60, BUTCH	BAILEY, NC
VHF 483	CLEVELAND, OHIO
HF 506, RAY	CALIF.
34-W-104, GARY	CALIF.
VHF 1590	
TXC 332	
24-W-1, JOHN	
HFA 2223, BOB	ALBERTSON, NC
FLA 1013	FLA.
HF 9133	FLA.
MUD SLINGER	OHIO
DAN, (NO HANDLE)	HALIFAX, NOVA SCOTIA
ONT 907, DAN	ONT. CANADA
32-W-47, BILL	
X 5355, JOHN	
2-W-27, JOE	
X 2968, CHARLES	
17 W 168, FRANK	
SB 766, BOB	
ISB 766, BOB	IOWA
ISB 882, RED	IOWA
FTC 794, BRUCE	
FTC 217,	MICH.
ISB 668, ERNIE	IOWA
UNIT 7	INDIANAPOLIA, IND.
TXC 332	MICH.
HF 9352, LEE	
TXC 526	
UNIT 10	WISC.
MR. PEPPER (ON SALT AND	
PEPPER BASE	KENOSHA, WISC
SAND LIZARD	
DOUBLE DUCE	CENTRAL MAINE
WOLVORENE	MONTREAL, CANADA
HF 7152, DUANE	ST. JOSEPH, MO.
HFX 8274, JOHN	KANSAS
GBA 22, ARNOLD	DODGE CITY, KANSAS
CHF 110, ED	NORTHERN ONTARIO
ARZ 410	ARIZONA

HOT DOG	WISC.
BUTTER MAN	WISC.
NORTH STAR	WISC.
HFX 9112	
6 W 154, ED	MASS.
6 W 140, PAUL	MASS
6 W 137B, ART	MASS
IRISHMAN	MIAMI, FLA.
JOLLY GREEN	MIAMI, FLA.
HF-188	FLA.
HF 4883	CALIF.
HFX 4617	CALIF.
HFA 2810	AMSTERDAM, NY
HFA 1401, HARLOD	ALA.
HF 6493, TED	
27 2 610, LEE	FLA.
6 W 145,	MASS.
HF 4454, TOM	MADISON, WISC.
HF 22161, ART	MADISON, WISC.
TP 15, EDDIE	HOUSTIN, TX.
HF 5705, JOE	LA GRANGE, NC
HFA 1152, BRAD	MISS.
X 8992	
HF 3581	
584	BOGOTA, COLUMBIA
HFX 675, LEE	MINN.
41 W 116, MERLE	MONTANA
4816, GRANT	KENNEWICK, WASH.
X 2635, MINNIE	
HF 3188	CONWAY, MICH.
HFX 3307	TEXAS
HFA 846	
UHF 82, RICHARD	NEW ORLEANS, LA.
HFX 4617, JOE	NEW ORLEANS, LA.
4 W 68	
HF 7979, JIM	TEXAS
HFX 7587, CHRIS	DUBUQUE, IOWA
BIG EYE IN THE	
SKY (BALOON)	FAYETTEVILLE, NC
25H, LEW	BERMUDA
HPW 1002, ROCKFISH	BERMUDA
301, JACK	BERMUDA

TRIPLE SEVEN   NOVA SCOTIA
4332,   IND.
4334,   IND.
4903   IND.
ANNA MARIE   IND.
OJR 406   FLA.
HF 4300, KEN   CLEAR WATER, FLA.
11 W 1015, JOE   MIDDLETOWN, NY
6 W 147, GEORGE   SPRINGFIELD, MASS
17 W 129
14 W 6   VERMONT
SNEEKIE PETE   WALLER, ARK.
                         President of "See More Nudist Colony"
UHF 16, EARL   LA.
HF 652
MO 454
27 W 1004   FLA.
HFA 7828
KEW 2580
24 W 66, KEVIN
HFA 2754, RICHARD
12 W 197, DICK
NA 291, AL
V 45 W, BOB
19 W 4559   FORT WAYNE, IND.
HFA 1586
NC 33
LSB 258
LSB 257
X 6993, JAY   BURLINGTON, IOWA
HFX 7504
HFX 1383
PUDDLE JUMPER   NOVA SCOTIA
21 W 5079
X 22 F, LARRY   IOWA
325, DON
NC 314
HFA 16, PAUL   RALEIGH, NC
2 W 929, LORRAINE
X 6812, DON   SPRINGFIELD, MASS.
HF 6991, JACK   PAMAMA CITY, FLA.
DU 35

HFA 505, JOE   LAKE WORTH, FLA.
HFA 1505, PEGGY   W. PALM BEACH, FLA.
27 W 1301   FLA.
NC 1242, DON
HF 5701, JIM   LAKE WORTH FLA.
                                    He issued my HFA-2223 number.

HF 5705, JOE   NC
CANDY MAN   RI.
SANDY   RI.
HF 9675
TAG A LONG   CONN.
RED HEAD   CONN.
WPO 1895   HARTFORD, CONN.
IC 77   CENTRAL ILL.
GCT 77   TEXAS
KWJ 3509
11 W 867   LONG ISLAND, NY
27 W 415   FLA.
6 W 106, MARK   SPRINGFIELD, MASS
9175, LOU   CONN.
X 7339, AMOS
CAPTAIN KIDD   NOVA SCOTIA
LITTLE ONE   MO.
466   PITCHFIELD, MASS
SEA GULL   ATLANTIC CITY, NJ
LITTLE RASCAL   MIAMI, FLA.
SKIPPER #2   MONTREAL
CRAZY HORSE   MONTREAL
251   ELIZABETHTOWN, NC
DOUBLE M   LA.
TIMBERWOLF   NOVA SCOTIA
JAIL BIRD   CANADA
10 W 1
NA 291   CANADA
NORTH ATLANTIC 292   CANADA, My first skip on Charlie
EL DORADO
COUNTRY BOY   TEXAS
UNIT 65   TEXAS
5 DOLLAR BILL   MISSOURI
MOUNTAIN BOY   OZARKS, MISSOURI
GRANDMA   LA.
TROPHY   LA.

THE PEANUT	MISSOURI
301	KENTUCKY
1439	KENTUCKY
688	MISSOURI
BUZZ SAW	WHEAT FIELDS OF KANSAS
101	ARK.
SW MISSOURI PINE TREE	MISSOURI
005	TENN.
PHANTOM	SW MISSOURI
HIGHWAY MAN	MISSOURI
BEE KEEPER	SW MISSOURI
UNIT 59	BERMUDA
MIGHTY MOBILE	BERMUDA
LUMBER JACK	BERMUDA
SILVER FOX	NOVA SCOTIA
RED ROOSTER	NOVA SCOTIA
UNIT 27	S. CAROLINA
LITTLE WAD	MASS.
MINI MO	MASS.
HOT ROD	HALIFAX, NOVA SCOTIA
WB	NOVA SCOTIA
MUD DOUBER	TEXAS
RED NECK	SW MISSOURI
8 BALL	WHEAT FIELDS OF KANSAS
21	MISS.
LAUNDRY MAN	MISS.
MOONDUSTER	KANSAS CITY
HORSE FLY	MISSOURI
NIGHT STALKER	SW MISSOURI
455	LA.
ICE MAN	SW MISSOURI
PUPPY TOES	S. CENTRAL LA.
313	ALA.
SWAMP RAT	MISS.
GRANDPA	LA.
MAIL BOX	OZARKS, ARK.
DIRTY DAGO	W. TENN.
PACK RAT	LA.
SWEETHEART	ALA.
WEST TENN. PLOW BOY MOUN-TAIN MAN	TENN HOT SPRINGS, ARK.
ARK. HILL BILLY	ARK.

KCV 7787	MISS.
MOTORCYCLE MAN	FORT SMITH, ARK.
UNIT 64	GATESVILLE, TX.
UNIT 95	BERMUDA
308	WISC.
255	WISC.
776	CHICAGO, ILL
SEA GULL	IND.
243	WISC
APACHE	DEARBORN, MICH.
BLACK HAWK	DEARBORN, MICH.
GUN RUNNER	MICH.
BIG MAN	MICH.
BLUE ANGEL	MICH.
SUPER FLY	CHICAGO
187	CHICAGO
T BONE	LAND OF LINCOLN
CRY BABY	LAND OF LINCOLN
007	SW MISSOURI
CARPET CLEANER	NEW BRUNSWICK, CANADA
ANNIE OAKLY	NEW BRUNSWICK, CANADA
PRETTY BOY	CANADA
SAGE	BRUNSWICK, MAINE
STUMP JUMPER	MAINE
GLOBEMASTER	NOVA SCOTIA
COAL MINER	NOVA SCOTIA
CCS 541	CANADA
DIGGER	ONT. CANADA
ORGAN GRINDER	ONT. CANADA
008	ONT. CANADA
TRIPLE W	MICH.
HAWKEYE	N. MICH.
389	CAPITOL CITY , MICH.
LUCKY 13	MICH.
351	LAND OF LINCOLN
OUTLAW	LONGVIEW, TX.
SAMMY DAVISFRAULINE	ST. LEWIS, MO.
BAT MAN	NOVA SCOTIA
HONEYBEE	NOVA SCOTIA
BIG DADDY	DIGBY, NOVA SCOTIA
POLAR BEAR	ST GEORGE, ONT.
FLASH	SW MISSOURI

COMPUTER	GLASGLO, NOVA SCOTIA
AM1960	MEDELLIN, COLUMBIA, S. AMERICA
BIG BLUE	ONT. CANADA
HAPPY HERMIT	SUDBURY, ONT.
GLOBEMASTER	WESTVILLE, NOVA SCOTIA
BROKEN ARROW	KANSAS CITY
DAGWOOD BASE	ST. LOUIS, MO.
PLOW BOY	IND.
POTAHAUNTAS	IND.
POWDER PUFF	ILL.
EAGLE CLAW	MINN.
CANADIAN SQUEAK	CANADA
TRAIL BOSS	MICH.
POLAR BEAR	ALASKA
YANKEE CONTROL	ILL.
COWBOY	ILL.
TEAKETTLE LADY	HOLLYWOOD, FLA.
COFFEE CUP	HOLLYWOOD, FLA.
SWORD FISH	HOLLYWOOD, FLA
MOUNTAIN BOY	MISSOURI
WHEELER DEALER	ARK.
BLUE BARON	MISSOURI
BLUE DIAMOND	ARK.
WIDOW	LA.
SWAMP BOY	LA.
JI	LA.
SKEETER BEATER	MISS.
SPARKIE	EAST TEXAS
624	MISS.
76	FLA.
351	LA.
531	LA.
6 PAK	MISS.
151	NEW ORLEANS
COUNTRY BOY	IND.
ANGEL	IND.
TOM CAT	ARK.
DOUBLE DUCE	IND.
FUNKY	IND.
BEER MAKER	CANADA
387	ST. LOUIS
505	MICH.

NIGHT STALKER	NY
347	ILL.
319	ILL.
IOWA CORN PICKER	IOWA
GREEN ONION	IOWA
DR 13	IOWA
PETER RABBIT	IOWA
CAROLINA TRANSPLANT	MISSOURI
SPUD	MISSOURI
663	MISSOURI
MODEL T	LA.
GRAVE DIGGER	LA.
238	LA.
133	MISS.
GRASS HOPPER	MISS.
RIFLEMAN	LA.
GATOR MAN	LA.
SKEETER	OK.
S. FLA. FARM BOY	FLA.
S. GEORGIA MOBILE	GA.
WITCH	GA.
PLAYBOY	OK.
GRANDPA	LA.
BOOGY BEACH MAN	ARK.